DIGNITY

DIGNITY

SEVEN STRATEGIES FOR CREATING AUTHENTIC COMMUNITY

BETH-SARAH WRIGHT, PhD

CHURCH
PUBLISHING
INCORPORATED

Church Publishing
19 East 34th Street
New York, NY 10016
www.churchpublishing.org

Cover design by Gillian Whiting
Typeset by Rose Design

A record of this book is available from the Library of Congress.
ISBN-13: 978-1-64065-333-7 (paperback)
ISBN-13: 978-1-64065-334-4 (ebook)

To my parents for always teaching us to see the dignity in others.

To my husband for always seeing in this work more than I could imagine.

To my children, may you always see yourselves the way God sees you.

Will you strive for justice and peace among all people, and respect the dignity of every human being?

—*The Book of Common Prayer*

CONTENTS

Foreword xi

Introduction: A New Way of Seeing xv

PART 1 / **THE STORY: AN INSTITUTIONAL TALE** 1

Points of View 3

    Jehan, the Student / 3

    Sofia, the Director of Student Life and Engagement / 6

    Susan, the Parent / 8

    Derek, the Teacher / 11

    Joshua, the School Headmaster / 14

    Joshua and the Manifesto / 17

The Story through the Dignity Lens 23

PART 2 / **THE DIGNITY LENS: SEVEN STRATEGIES** 25

Diversity 27

Identity 36

Growth 44

Nurture 51

Integrity 58

Transparency 63

Yield 68

Summary 73

Epilogue: What about Me?

Imagine Your Life Based on DIGNITY 81

Look closely at the present you are constructing. It should look like the future you are dreaming.

—*Alice Walker*

LOOK AGAIN

A new way of being. Of thinking.

At last a lens to dream a little

A new way of seeing.

Look again.

Gather up the courage.

Be vulnerable.

Be hopeful.

Swallow your fear.

It only takes one change to grow in capacity.

Expand your diaphragm of vulnerability and exhale a new thought.

No guilt. No shame. No condemnation.

Look again, I ask.

Look again!

—*Beth-Sarah Wright, PhD*

FOREWORD

This concept of DIGNITY as a set of strategies was birthed out of my experience as the director of enrollment management at the largest Episcopal parish day school in the nation, Holy Innocents' Episcopal School (HIES) in Atlanta, Georgia. In this capacity, a large part of my work was communicating our school's story/purpose/identity in a compelling and authentic way to the wider community to attract more students and families to apply and ultimately enroll at our school. I exhorted my team and the HIES community to "Know the Mission and Tell the Story," a succinct and clear way to know who we say we are and to communicate that mission through storytelling enriched by our own individual experiences and intimate knowledge.

But as we progressed in this work, I realized this was easier said than done. Did everyone know and fully comprehend the HIES mission? What about internalizing that mission, to make it their own? What parts of the story were being told? What parts remained untold? Was our lived story an accurate reflection of our stated mission? I discovered there were gaps, and I found myself shifting to strategically close those gaps and to actually make HIES a more authentic community, where our mission and our story actually align. DIGNITY was born out of that work.

I have used this framework for four years now in the admissions process, in how we identify mission-aligned students, and as a tool for the board of trustees in addressing the strategic goal of living more into our Episcopal identity as an inclusive and welcoming environment where the dignity of all students, faculty, parents, and staff is valued and nurtured. As a result, I have also shared this with the faculty and my cohort at the Rossier School of Education at the University of Southern California, where I received a certificate in Leadership in Enrollment Management. There, it was positively embraced and found to be adaptable to many situations facing education around enrollment, admissions, branding, leadership, aligning with core purpose, and identity. It soon became clear to me that the DIGNITY concept is translatable and useful for different types of communities as they too work to develop, articulate, and live out a corporate purpose and identity, all while maintaining dignity at the core.

While birthed in this educational setting, DIGNITY has actually been influenced by and is inextricably tied to my life experiences as a trained anthropologist and ethnographer, a peripatetic, a survivor of depression and mental health advocate, a wife, mother and Christian. I have written four books on topics that at their core are about dignity and authenticity. Two are specifically on my mental health journey from diagnosis to healing of depression, which spawned a relationship as an assistant adjunct professorship in the department of psychiatry at Emory University's School of Medicine. One, a spiritual novel rooted in the life stories of three generations of women in a transnational context spanning the Caribbean, UK, and USA, and one a book of meditations centered around the convergence of the Nicene Creed, Jesus's life story, and my own life story. As a public and inspirational speaker, I have addressed many communities—from churches, to theological and medical students, to mental health communities, to schools—to inspire people to tell their stories and ultimately to see the dignity in their stories and in the world, to bring about healing, wholeness, and authentic living. Without specific intention, I have been massaging this concept of dignity for many years and offer it now as a tool and resource for communities to reflect, embrace, and enact new ways of seeing and being in this world, on their way to becoming communities of integrity and wholeness.

Dignity remains at the core of just about everything. And yet, every day, people's dignity is violated in small and large ways. It's the thing we all share, we all have in common, and we all feel deeply. And we rarely see it or acknowledge it. It is my hope for us to see it more. To remember that it connects us. And that if we remain aware of dignity in our daily lives, our families, and our work, not only will we live more authentically, closer to the dream God has for us as individuals, but our communities and organizations will also be more impactful, efficacious, and productive. With dignity, there will be more opened hearts for loving, opened hands for connecting, opened arms for embracing, opened doors and borders for welcoming, opened eyes for seeing, and opened minds for understanding. Ultimately, "[we] can develop a healthy, robust community that lives right with God and enjoy its results *only* if you do the hard work of getting along with each other, treating each other with dignity and honor."[1]

I write this foreword presently during the unprecedented global pandemic of COVID-19. As a result of this crisis, communities

---

1. James 3:17, Eugene H. Peterson, *The Message: The Bible in Contemporary Language* (Colorado Springs: NavPress, 2002).

and organizations all over the world have been forced in one way or another to radically adapt in these unpredictable and uncertain circumstances. While some may be taking advantage of the ocean of human fear and anxiety we are all experiencing, others are using this time to live deeper into the words they profess about their mission and identity, infusing their purpose with new meaning to magnify the focus on human dignity. They are radically and rapidly tackling tough challenges and innovating solutions, perhaps never even imagined before. It is a laboratory for DIGNITY work. We do not know what the future holds, but as we forge ahead, I profoundly hope we don't ever let go of this urgency to transform and adapt, to evolve and reveal new ways of being, authentically and with integrity, and always with human dignity at the center.

INTRODUCTION

A NEW WAY OF SEEING

It's not what you look at that matters . . . it's what you see.
—*Henry David Thoreau*

O n a car ride home while snacking on strawberries in the back seat, my youngest son, Moses, then about eight years old, with the glee of a newfound discovery, squealed, "Look, Mommy!" I could see him in the rearview mirror, hand outstretched with a couple of strawberry leaves in his sticky fingers. "Look! It's a heart!" Indeed, the way he held those leaves formed a perfectly shaped heart. He said with such pride, "I can see the love in everything." That started his and my own adventures into seeing hearts in just about everything, from a discarded piece of plastic on the ground to old chewing gum on the sidewalk. What was so instructive for me, though, in his childhood innocence, was his ability to look at what he held in his fingers and to look again to see something completely new, meaningful, and equally real. The leaves, in effect, did transform in his eyes to a symmetrical heart. It dawned on me that the openness and willingness to see beyond is an invitation to us all to look more deeply into the things in front of us, to see fertile potential and fresh possibilities, to articulate and share them and then to bring them into reality. Imagine what it would be like to bring this openness and willingness to see differently to our work.

For years now, I've been on a mission to encourage people to see beyond their initial, often limiting observations, to look again and see immense possibilities, especially when tasked with imagining solutions to tough problems. Most recently, I find myself focused on the strategic work of institutions, more specifically independent schools, where there exists a persistent challenge of closing the gap between who we say we are as articulated in our institutional identities and who we actually are, in our lived reality. The invitation in this book is to close that gap and become more authentic communities by looking again at who we say we are and mining that to see new competencies, new capacities, new acumen, new skills to ultimately become who we say we are. This book was written particularly for people at any level of institutional life, no matter the position or the type of institution—educational, religious, entrepreneurial, social, or professional. We all share this work regardless of occupational status or rank. We all have institutional power and purpose by virtue of belonging to and working on behalf of the institution. In schools for example, the students, the teachers and faculty, the leadership team, the facilities team, the coaches, the parents, the board of trustees all share in the work to become more authentic and all have the power to enact change and move the institution toward its aspirational identity. Yet we are all different and as we work together to become a more authentic community, we must be open to recognizing the vast potential and value we all bring to enact transformational change, beyond our differences and inherently rooted in our humanity.

As the director of admissions and enrollment management at an independent Episcopal school in Atlanta, Georgia, I was tasked to partner with a board of trustees objective, "to increase diversity in the student body, faculty and board of trustees," arguably an objective many independent schools aspire to, yet struggle with, in their "diversity statements" and/or institutional identities. Again, the question of visibility, what you see, persists. In fact, it fundamentally undergirds the work of this objective. Where for some, the board objective is seen through the lens of demographics, I ultimately proposed that this work would be more effective and sustainable if we approached it through the lens of human potential and human dignity. As I began to address this work, I rediscovered in the founding principles of Episcopal schools a commitment to living out a single mission, a question. This question unlocked for me the challenge of how we as an institution could more authentically live out, not only this board objective, but frankly just about any strategic objective. "Will you strive to . . . respect the dignity of every human being?"[1] This single question reframed the objective by surfacing new questions to grapple with. Can we see this demographic change as an opportunity for more human connection and increased learning rather than a box to be checked? Can we see this objective as an occasion to more authentically be who we say we are as an educational institution? Can we see beyond our presumptions about students of different educational, socioeconomic, ethnic, or cultural backgrounds to see our shared dignity? Can we see beyond the loss we think we'll experience by including new people? "The

---

1. Baptismal Covenant of the Episcopal Church, *The Book of Common Prayer and Administration of the Sacraments and Other Rites and Ceremonies of the Church: Together with the Psalter or Psalms of David According to the Use of the Episcopal Church* (New York: Seabury Press, 1979), 305.

real voyage of discovery consists not in seeking new lands but in seeing with new eyes."[2] Discovering that question shifted everything: how we connect to or "buy in" to the solution, whose work it is, clarifying the purpose, identifying the loss and the gain. Ultimately, the focus on dignity became the genesis for my work and this book. It frames an approach that shifts any strategic conversation from what we see to how we see.

What is remarkable about this provocative question is that it does not ask to "tolerate," "work with," or "lead" others; it does not ask "to agree with" or "be kind to," "be polite to" or even "love" every human being. It asks to respect their dignity. *Respect.* From the Latin root word *specere*, to look, and *re*, again, "re-spect" literally means to look again. It is to look at a person and to be present to the many assumptions, preconceived notions, or biases we have and to look again, to see new possibilities and new understandings. Additionally, to "strive" clearly intimates that there is a process that requires effort, intentionality, and innovation. It suggests progress and movement towards an aspiration or attainable dream, if you will, rather than a clear-cut solution. The persistent challenge with having a dream is the potential of a gap between the reality and the dream. It is in bridging the gap that I am most invested.

Being open to new ways of being and understanding, to living out our purpose more authentically, is essential work for our institutions. It is part imagination, part capacity-building, part urgent, and part non-negotiable. We must increase our capacity and comfort with this idea of looking again, or re-specting, the people we work with, the people we serve, the work we do, and even the

---

2. Marcel Proust, *The Captive; The Fugitive*, trans. and ed. C. J. Scott-Moncrieff (New York: Modern Library, 1993), 343, paraphrase.

challenges we face. This notion of "re-specting dignity" may challenge more popular understandings of these words. Donna Hicks, in her seminal text on dignity, offers a distinction between dignity and respect, saying, "Respect is different. Although everyone has dignity, not everyone deserves respect. Respect must be earned."[3] To clarify, in this book, I am using the etymological meaning of "respect," the act of looking again, which is not due only to certain individuals or situations. Inspired by the question "Will you strive to respect the dignity of *every* human being?" the invitation to re-spect, look again, is not limited to those whose behavior we admire or who have accomplished extraordinary achievements. It is also not limited to those challenges that we feel comfortable addressing, or that we feel connected to. Regardless of who we are looking at or their behavior or external appearance; regardless of the difficulty or discomfort of a particular challenge in our work, we are called to look again and see their inherent worth and value, their dignity.

After all, dignity itself is unwavering and immovable. We all have it, and naturally yearn for it to be recognized. *Thymos* is the part of the soul that craves recognition of dignity, and author Francis Fukuyama argues that the demand for equal recognition of dignity is the master concept underlying much of what is going on in world politics today.[4] In fact, he argues that entire countries can feel disrespected, which can power aggressive nationalism. Dignity transcends all barriers. The desire for dignity and respect is universal and powerful, a motivating force behind all human interaction. Learning about dignity is no longer an option. It is

---

3. Donna Hicks, *Leading with Dignity: How to Create a Culture That Brings Out the Best in People* (New Haven: Yale University Press, 2019), 2.

4. Francis Fukuyama, *Identity: The Demand for Dignity and the Politics of Resentment* (New York: Farrar, Straus and Giroux, 2018), xiii.

a human imperative. If we remain ignorant of the essential role it plays, there is little hope of seeing appreciable change in our world. To see the dignity in every human being is to see beyond that which we believe is real—which are only figments of our manipulated, maneuvered, and molded imaginations anyway—to see what is truly real, the omnipresent capacity and potential in each of us. That intangible thing that makes us all human. Regardless of its outward manifestations, our dignity knows we are made for more; it thirsts for knowledge and for discovering the truth; it seeks freedom and has at its core the desire to be seen as fully human. Interestingly, *thymos*, the very part of the soul that yearns for recognition of dignity, in other Greek contexts is defined as "heart." Could it be that my son's desire to see "hearts" in everything is emblematic for us to look again at the dignity in our communities, our organizations, our institutional identities? Yes. For the mere fact that our institutions rely on human connection, to see the "heart" or dignity in our work is pivotal in our purpose to live out our aspirations and thrive as institutions of integrity.

But how? How can we as an institution practically shift the way we see? I offer the DIGNITY lens: a transformative, comprehensive set of seven strategies, each denoted by a letter in the word dignity, to look deep into our aspirational challenges and excavate means of bridging the gap between our aspirations and current reality. Diversity. Identity. Growth. Nurture. Integrity. Yield. These seven tenets are not linear and can start at any point; they can be implemented by anyone, at any time, in any place. This work is not relegated to people with formal authority or experts in our communities. This is shared work; the solutions come from us, the institutional corpus. Anyone in the system can take up DIGNITY work. By virtue of our institutional affiliation, we have been entrusted by the institution with the power to make change. We have the power to shift our way of seeing and thinking in line with the community identity and community aspirations. Espousing DIGNITY as a strategic lens, shifts our work from fulfilling tasks to leveraging our power to maximize institutional identity, with integrity. As uncomfortable and challenging as it may be to see and think in new ways, it is crucial to this work. In DIGNITY, we can't escape the work, no matter how uncomfortable it is. In DIGNITY, we lean into discomfort and grow in our capacity to be comfortable with discomfort. Along with this new way of seeing is an accompanying attitude. It is not one of confidence and skill, rather it is power brought on by curiosity—asking questions and solving for the problem at hand. DIGNITY gives us the tools to accomplish the goal and makes it much easier for us to invite others to engage in this work, looking at profound problems and their solutions in new ways.

All parts of the DIGNITY lens are interconnected and the work is rendered less effective if each part is not engaged. Each strategy asks a series of questions and provides opportunities to be reflective about who we are and what we value; about our capacity for growth and loss; about our capacity to have tough conversations and make informed decisions and choices; about working with others despite our differences; about communicating with transparency and holding ourselves accountable to our community ideals.

The DIGNITY lens is most useful when addressing the types of challenges that require attitudinal, cultural, and identity shifts. They require changes in capacities and competencies. These challenges are often persistent and difficult to crack. The challenges that affect us on a visceral level. The types of challenges to which there is no immediate and apparent solution, where the issue repeatedly surfaces because we can't quite get a handle on it. DIGNITY work takes time. It is characterized by progress and striving. There are no quick fixes. In DIGNITY work, the challenges are not clear and they require learning and new competencies. They are comprehensive in nature and require several different perspectives. These challenges are potentially explosive because they affect us on a deep emotional level, where identity, attitudes, behaviors, and, indeed, dignity reside. Because these challenges live where dignity resides, they require dignity work to be solved. Leadership expert Ron Heifetz describes these problems as adaptive challenges. Adaptive challenges "live in peoples' hearts and stomachs. They are about values, loyalties and beliefs."[5]

The DIGNITY lens allows us to see these potentially gut-wrenching challenges differently, as holding great potential for the institution. It enables us to confront these tough issues and begin to conceive of sustainable and transformative solutions. "Not everything that is faced can be changed, but nothing can be changed if it not faced," wrote the late James Baldwin.[6] The DIGNITY lens allows us to see the matter as an opportunity for creative thinking, for innovative solutions, for mobilizing and including different people across boundaries around this one collective aspiration. DIGNITY is the lens and framework, a set of strategies with which to achieve that ultimate goal. Becoming an authentic community means aligning what you do with who you say you are.

No one ever said it would be easy. DIGNITY work is hard but not impossible. DIGNITY work is not about getting along or

---

5. Ed O'Malley and Amanda Cebula, *Your Leadership Edge: Lead Anytime, Anywhere* (Wichita, KS: Kansas Leadership Center Press, 2015), 14.

6. *I Am Not Your Negro*, directed by Raoul Peck (2016; New York: Magnolia Pictures) based on James Baldwin's unfinished manuscript *Remember This House*.

keeping the peace or being polite. It is not a result of a political, religious, or even moral imperative. It is not about recognizing difference and engaging in a potentially paralyzing world of political correctness. It is not silencing our opinions, assumptions, or beliefs for the sake of not being offensive. It is not walking on eggshells, or fostering an environment of guilt, blame, or shame. It is none of these things. Rather, DIGNITY work is difficult, uncomfortable, self-reflective, and comprehensive work that cultivates an environment of integrity and authenticity.

My hope in writing this book is to put the word "dignity" in more mouths every day, where people brainstorming around the office or tackling a tough problem at work ask, "Well, what about the 'G' in DIGNITY? What is the opportunity to grow here?" Or "That question is really about the 'I' in DIGNITY . . . how is the new initiative connected to our identity?" Not only will the word "dignity" be in more mouths, but the way we see will be colored by dignity. I hope for more communities to see the capacity and potential in our communities for change and for becoming more authentic. Authentic communities make up more of an authentic world, where what we say and what we do align.

I will introduce the DIGNITY lens through the telling of a story. It is a fictional account of an imaginary school, grappling with its aspirational identity and its current reality. It centers around a specific incident seen from multiple lens and points of view within that community. My intention is for you to get lost in the intricacies and details of the story, and see in it, dimensions of your own community. Ultimately, when it comes to becoming more authentic, we all struggle with common concerns, common obstacles, and common approaches to solutions. The story is just a starting point. Be open. Be curious. Embrace a new way of seeing and see your community thrive!

PART 1

THE STORY:
AN INSTITUTIONAL TALE

POINTS OF VIEW

Jehan, the Student

Could my senior year of high school begin any better? The director of student life and engagement just asked me to read a passage in the upcoming first ever all-school assembly! I was so excited to be a part of it. In addition to planning for senior week and my last homecoming and all the "lasts" I was about to experience this year, here was a "first" and it was like icing on the cake. It was an honor to be asked to participate in a school event, but to be asked to read a passage from my family's holy book, the Quran, made it all the more special.

I always loved sharing parts of my life that my friends at school rarely saw or knew about. I loved sharing my mother's delicious Persian food and I loved teaching a word or two of Farsi to my friends. I remembered back in tenth grade, in our World Religions class, the whole class visited several holy places of worship: Christian churches, a Jewish temple, and a mosque in the city. I had only attended the mosque a few times in my life, but I was familiar enough with it to have some inside knowledge to share. I was so proud and excited to share what I knew, from how to put on the scarves to cover our heads and shoulders to how to kneel and pray. And now, to share this part of me and my family with my friends and the entire school was a thrill. I decided I would not only read the passage in English but read it in my parents' language of Farsi as well!

But first I had to translate it. I called my aunt first, because I knew she was very spiritual and would help me with an accurate translation. We worked on it for a few hours and I practiced to get the pronunciations correct. Even though I grew up hearing and speaking Farsi at home, English is my first language so I wanted to be sure I was saying the words correctly, not that many people would understand what I was saying! As far as I knew, my family were one of very few Persian families at school. I may look different from most of the students there, but this was my school, my home. Even being one of very few Muslims at this private school was not an issue. I grew up here—I attended this school since I was four years old. I may have been in the ethnic minority, but I always felt like I belonged. This school was my family.

We had never had an all-school assembly before. Ms. Sofia told me she wanted the assembly to be both entertaining and thought-provoking. A time for us to think ethically and to celebrate values that connected us, not that divided us. We always said we were an inclusive school, and that we had created an environment where everybody was valued, affirmed, and included, so the idea of this all-school assembly sounded right. In fact, one of the rules for the student clubs at our school was that they could not be exclusive; everyone had to have the option to join. Even though we were not a religiously affiliated school, we had guest speakers in our classes sometimes, a rabbi or a Baptist minister, and we recognized when our friends were celebrating Rosh Hashanah or Hanukkah, and they were invited to share their family traditions with the class. I didn't think anything of it to be invited to read from the Quran at this assembly.

I felt so proud of my school to be asked to read from the Quran in the midst of what the world seemed to be thinking about Muslims. You couldn't turn on the television or listen to the radio without hearing something about the "Muslim ban" or that Muslims were hate mongering or violent and that beheadings were a part of the faith. I personally didn't feel questioned about my faith at school, as many of my friends and teachers probably didn't even know or care that my family was Muslim. I still felt a certain pride, though, in being able to celebrate this part of me with my school family. Of all places, this was the safest and most accepting place to do this.

I walked to the lectern that day, armed with the confidence I had practiced each word and I could practically recite the passage by heart. The words were so beautiful, lyrical and full of meaning. "So, compete with each other in doing good. Every one of you will return to God, and God will teach you about the differences of humanity. . . ." They rolled off my tongue with the ease of exhaling. Like a sweet breath, they floated into the air and landed on the ears of my friends and teachers—people I had known almost all my life. I would never have imagined in a thousand years, after I stepped down from that lectern, the cruel and hurtful words that flew in my direction and how quickly those people would change how they saw me after those four minutes of our lives together.

Sofia, the Director of Student Life and Engagement

I left my new boss's office feeling so empowered and focused on the task at hand. This was only my second month in this position as the director of student life and engagement, a position that called for me to oversee student activity and engagement and to help cultivate a learning community where each student felt they truly and fully belonged, without leaving any part of themselves outside of these doors. The most involved aspect of this work was to conceive of weekly assemblies and programming, including this new all-school assembly of fourteen hundred students from three-year-olds to high school seniors. I was determined and excited to make this a success. To prepare, I sat with the head of school to get a sense of his vision for the initial gathering: to create an event that celebrated our school identity and embraced and affirmed the rich diversity in the student body. Simple, right? Yes, but also a great challenge. I would never have anticipated the firestorm that was about to be ignited by the simple choices we made to accomplish the stated mission.

The mission of our school had always been clearly articulated to me. In my job interview, I answered many questions about how to navigate ensuring all students were included and able to flourish. How would you cultivate an environment where all students are affirmed and included? How do you include the Hindu student, affirm the physically disabled student and celebrate the Asian American student? How do you create an inclusive space where all feel a sense of belonging? This intentional hospitality and welcome was evident in all the literature the school shared with prospective families and on their website. Regardless of my familiarity with this worthy aspiration, planning this service still presented new territory for me. How do I elegantly include a celebration of diversity into this assembly to create an entertaining, provocative, and school-spirited experience? My first draft was sent back to me for revision. It leaned too heavily on the school's historical traditions and did not yet reflect the affirmation of some newer narratives of inclusion and affirmation. This happened not once, not twice, but three times! I really appreciated the intentionality. It just wasn't enough to say it: the assembly had to reflect it.

I admit I was stumped at first. Then Jehan stopped by my office to ask about a homecoming event she was planning and the lightbulb exploded! As she was talking, I noticed her bracelet with a crescent and star symbol on it. I asked if she was Muslim and when she said yes, it all came together in my head. Have a few students share something from their faith—especially students of the three Abrahamic faiths, Christianity, Islam, and Judaism, which share the same root. That seemed a great way to have the students more involved and to raise up some values that connect us. It just opened up the possibilities. Jehan's excitement and enthusiasm was tremendous. I reworked the draft and this time, it was approved. Yes, it captured the essence of the school mission. Yes, it was a celebration and reflection of our diverse student body. Yes, it was all this and yet, it was a minefield of explosives I never anticipated.

Susan, the Parent

What has happened to my school? It's been nearly fourteen years now that my children have attended here. Fourteen years of volunteering endlessly in the parents' association. Fourteen years of enduring painfully long carpool lines on hot afternoons and frigid mornings. Fourteen years of annual tuition raises and annual fundraisers. I'd do it all over again because I love this school and the education it has given my children, but after yesterday's all-school assembly, my love for this school has been challenged in ways I hadn't thought possible.

I sought out this school for my first child because it captured all I hoped for in an educational environment. I wanted a sense of community with like-minded friends. A place where my children would be known and nurtured as they matured academically and socially. I wanted a place that fostered decent, good kids, who were respectful and kind. And I wanted a school with some spiritual or character-building component. This school was not religiously affiliated, but it did focus on the social and emotional development of students. It offered opportunities for them to develop and mature into good citizens, good human beings, the values that we tried to instill in our home. I wanted a school that spoke about values and ethics and making good choices. It was simple, really, and I have been more than happy with the ways in which the school has achieved this. Happy up until yesterday when I was completely dumbfounded by the choice to include a reading from the Quran at the assembly.

Don't get me wrong, I am not intolerant of different faiths. In fact, I've known the young lady who read at the assembly since she was in preschool. She is friends with my daughter. I knew her parents were Middle Eastern but I did not know they were

Muslim. Why would the school put Jehan in such an awkward situation? And who is this new director of student life anyway? What was she thinking? Why is she trying to change the nature of this school? To read from the Quran in a traditional Judeo-Christian school in the United States? Why? Why would they do that? Jehan is of course free to practice her own faith but why here? Why now? Why in this school? Why must we be exposed to a belief so different from what the majority of us believe as Christians? A faith that espouses violence and terrorism? As a country, we are already making a statement about this faith and its practitioners right now with the executive order. And here at my children's school we are going in a completely different direction . . . actually embracing and extolling this religion. Don't they remember 9/11? I am completely astounded and frankly angered by the whole thing.

There is a time and a space for the study of different religions. I am not against that at all. Creating an inclusive environment for the students is a noble undertaking, but the means by which this goal is being pursued by this director of student life and administration is deeply flawed. When did it become acceptable to include readings from the Muslim faith in a gathering with impressionable children? What about our youngest children who lack the cognitive ability to discern what is happening? How are they supposed to know what is the truth and what is not? What about them?

Is this what the administration believes must be done to create an "inclusive and welcoming" environment? I know we are a welcoming environment. As a practicing Christian, I have never felt excluded at this school that does not espouse any particular faith. Each year, a few new students are admitted who come from different schools and areas and backgrounds. I know we have a financial aid program—I think I even contribute to that each year. We are an inclusive and welcoming school. But to have our children exposed to this religion in a traditional school is ridiculous and misinformed. To be exposed to readings affirming beliefs of Islam? Is this where we're headed? Soon our children will be reciting and singing songs from all these traditions . . . Judaism, Islam, Buddhism, New Age, even atheism!

This is truly unacceptable. I know other parents have the same concerns. I must get to the bottom of this abrupt and secretive agenda by the school leadership to implement these new changes and ultimately shift this school from its Judeo-Christian roots to one that embraces all religions without thought. And if they don't stop this nonsense now, I will contemplate leaving this school.

Derek, the Teacher

It was supposed to have been a glorious coming together of the entire student body and faculty in our inaugural annual all-school assembly. I couldn't believe it took such a negative turn. It's all my eleventh-grade Religion class wanted to talk about today. The energy was palpable. Their usual apathy had been replaced with a fierce urgency to discuss the incidents of the day before. Many of them sat at their desks straining like bulls waiting for the buzzer to sound and the bucking chute gate to fling open. Their euphemistic question: Should readings from *any* religious text—for example, the Quran—be included in all-school assembly? Their actual question: Why is our school changing so drastically and trying to shove Islam down our throats?

How was I going to have this class discussion in light of what I had witnessed yesterday? The surprise. The looks of disgust. How was I going to control the blazing temperature in the room? In the classroom were seventeen-year-olds who had gone home the day before to their predominantly white, Christian, conservative-leaning, and wealthy homes and to parents who no doubt had something to say about what went down at the assembly. Now, they were charged up and ready, alongside the very student who had read a passage from the Quran, her family's religious text, at the school's invitation no less. A student who had been at this private school since pre-kindergarten, surrounded by friends she'd known almost all her life. Some in support of what happened. Others confused and angry. I didn't know what would happen if I opened the doors for conversation in the classroom. The emotions. The rhetoric. The blame. Would they offend her? Her parents? Would they be unkind?

I have been a teacher at this school for many years without this sort of issue presenting a problem. To discuss issues like these in the abstract was one thing, but to face the raw reality of it right here in the classroom was something altogether different. Not coincidentally, the cloud of opinions about the recent presidential Executive Order 13769, popularly known as the Muslim ban, hung heavy in the air. I didn't know how much of my own feelings I could contain. Should I share what I feel? I still had a responsibility to teach this class in the midst of all this and I was feeling overwhelmed. I felt unprepared and to say I was uncomfortable was an understatement. Honestly, I was scared. Deathly afraid.

Maybe I could run down the hall and get the director of student life and engagement to come and explain all this. She would do a much better job at this anyway. Or would she? She was implicated as the instigator of all this. Maybe I could call Jehan's parents and invite them in to share their thoughts. I knew them. They were often on campus for events. Surely, they would know what to say and how to say it. The students would be more respectful, and their daughter would feel safe. That's it! That's the answer. But then, what would I say to them? "Mr. and Mrs. Ahman, would you come to my class to explain your entire faith to a bunch of eleventh graders . . . oh, and also explain why some Muslims might use suicide bombs and also what are your thoughts about the Muslim ban?" Yep. That would really sound welcoming and open-minded and not in the least bit insensitive.

I was at my wits' end. I did what I felt most comfortable doing in that moment: I shifted the conversation and went on to the next chapter in the book, which fortunately had nothing to do with the subject at hand. I went home feeling like a coward. My wife knew exactly what my face meant.

"Honey, you've always been able to make sense of things and to explain them in a simple and effective way. Aren't you the teacher?" Yes. "Aren't you in control of the class?" Yes. "Would you ever let anything happen to Jehan?" No. "Isn't it your responsibility to encourage critical thinking?"

Yes . . . but how? How can I control what they will say or how they will say it? They're just seventeen-year-olds. "Come on, Derek, how did you all handle it in grad school? Haven't you always done that? Find a way. Find a way that works in this context. This is your chance to truly be the teacher. Step out, Derek, and tell a story. You never know what you're capable of unless you try. They won't be able to have a critical conversation if you are not able to model one. And I know you can do that. Do it now, Derek. Find a way."

Joshua, the School Headmaster

Did I make the right choice? Is this the school my family and I thought it was? I am stunned by the vitriolic response to the all-school assembly. It's been three years now that I've been at the helm of this large private school. I was thrilled at the opportunity to maintain the legacy of this well-established school and lead it into the next years of excellence. I was struck in the search process by two primary features about this school: First, its commitment to creating an atmosphere that encouraged students to excel in multiple avenues, and second, its stated mission of fostering an inclusive and healthy learning environment where the unique abilities of each individual are recognized and affirmed. In my previous schools, I had seldom witnessed this intentional pluralism and welcome. It was a refreshing joy to see this openness in community. At least this is what I had understood of the ethos of this school, until the fallout from the recent all-school assembly.

All I could think about in the post-assembly flurry of emotions, was "aren't we an inclusive school? Don't we say we appreciate and celebrate the uniqueness of each individual in this community? Aren't we doing what we say we're doing?" I kept coming back to the basics. Back to who I thought we were as a school. In a matter of days following the assembly, I heard from both disgruntled parents and supportive parents, hurt students, skeptical, committed, and even regretful colleagues . . . so many emotional responses to apparently the most powerful four minutes in a ninety-minute assembly. The emails and text messages were pouring in. Some in stalwart support, others questioning my leadership and my attempt to lean into, what I thought was, a well-established path of inclusivity and acceptance in the school. I was knocked back on my heels. Was this the same nurturing community of far-reaching welcome I had chosen to join just three years ago?

We needed to do some damage control. Anonymous and not-so-anonymous emails circulated following the assembly, soliciting support for a petition to challenge the school and its leadership. I knew these people. We had shared meals together. Sat beside each other at football and baseball games. Listened to our children perform together at orchestra and band concerts. Yet, here we were in a sea of misunderstanding, fear, and confusion. I know these folks weren't speaking out of evil or maliciousness, but rather from deep concern, albeit misinformed, for their children. While I respected their concern, I had to find a way to control the woundedness in the system. It seemed to me that the only way to quell these aberrant voices was to remind them of who we as a school claimed to be.

The board of trustees' strategic plan, in place prior to my arrival, had as its primary pillar to "live into our educational identity." I now see that this seemingly perfunctory and even token objective was not so simple. Rather, upon reflection, it was actually coming from a deeper systemic omission that had not been appropriately tended to over the years. The best way I understood it was by remembering my teen years and my first car. I was so ignorant about car mechanics and so wanted to cut costs that I never paid attention to the routine maintenance of the car. I wasn't a reckless or irresponsible driver; I just never maintained the car. Before I knew it, I had a major system failure on Highway 10 and that was the end of my first car. What was happening here was deferred maintenance around who we were and who we claim to be. I remembered

Langston Hughes's prophetic words when he asked, "What happens to a dream deferred? . . . Does it dry up like a raisin in the sun? . . . Maybe it just sags like a heavy load. Or does it explode?" And explode it did, right before my eyes.

Joshua and the Manifesto

So how to calm the turbulent waters? How to mitigate the threat of parents leaving the school or taking this to the media? How to assuage their genuine fears? By communicating clearly with the community, reiterating the core tenants of our identity to cultivate an atmosphere of openness and listening and bravery so that all voices could be heard.

At first, I simply opened my door, metaphorically and physically. It was an unabashed invitation to listen. To be open to hearing the worst possible interpretation of what others experienced and to simply sit with their pain. They felt blindsided. "That this was an abrupt change in our philosophy and identity as a school." There was mistrust, and the illogical reasoning morphed into absurd accusations about my integrity and my "devious plan" to "take the school into new directions" that apparently conflicted with *their* understanding of the school.

I decided I had to go back to basics. I had to remind the community of who we were and why we were refining the mission and infusing it with new meaning. I had to remind them of the comprehensive strategic plan, which they had contributed to and helped to devise, ironically, with its first objective being to live into our educational identity. I wanted to remind them of why we believed that a diverse and inclusive learning environment was the linchpin in providing a quality education and that respect and empathy for others are fundamental in creating confident, equipped global citizens. This was our understanding of educating the whole child.

Even though this incident had spewed a tornado of questions and concerns about the direction of the school, its identity, and my leadership, I had to realize that this whirlwind was limited in its scope and only occupied a small area of the much more expansive landscape. Loud? Yes. Disturbing? Yes. But representative of the entire community? No. The most effective way of speaking to that minority without identifying them specifically, and to reeducate the entire community about our identity, was to write a declaration that judiciously addressed the concerns some parents, students, and faculty had voiced.

I gathered information and data and research. How can I balance education and correction? Would my emotions bleed through the words on the page? What will the tone be? Will my words empower those vociferous voices or subdue them?

I began:

> Today we are living in an historical moment, when many questions and opinions about the state and direction of our country abound, especially as it regards people of different beliefs and faith backgrounds. As an educational community we too must question and think critically and be curious about all perspectives. Within these doors we must stand firm in our identity of inclusivity, and simultaneously with respect and intellectual curiosity engage with the richness of experiences in the world. We are a community that appreciates the bountiful diversity of humanity and can elegantly hold in balance its complexities and values as we seek to gain new understanding of our common life. This goal is not one in response to political agendas but a long-lasting deep commitment to academic excellence evident in our founding DNA. Knowing that conversations and questions will arise, we encourage you to embrace these time-honored values and engage in meaningful and open-minded exchange. Together, our community is able to build bridges and be united in love and commitment to a common purpose.

The Backstory

When it was founded sixty-five years ago by a small group of innovative educational leaders, the vision was to create a school to develop the imagination and intellectual curiosity of each student, in an inclusive and healthy learning environment, so that each child's abilities and stories would be recognized and affirmed and live into their full potential. As such, they hoped that each student would feel a sense of belonging and place in this environment. Focused on the development of the whole child, they aimed to expose students to as many disciplines and opportunities as possible so that their imaginations would be inspired and they could develop interests and passions, without sacrificing one for the other.

Over the years, with each head, the school had developed and matured, growing in size and adjusting to technological and pedagogical innovations.

Joshua began his tenure near the end of a ten-year strategic plan, which had, in addition to pillars around academic excellence, quality faculty, and campus renovation, a pillar devoted to living into its educational identity.

Maintaining the identity of an institution is, in many ways, a soft feature, seemingly not bound to numbers and outcomes but rather to feelings and more nebulous ideas and emotions. In terms of this goal, some of the stated outcomes were "to increase diversity of students and faculty," "increase the financial aid for socioeconomic diversity," "create a non-discriminatory policy and approach across an array of domains from admissions, to student life, to athletics," "create a full-time position for a person dedicated to the life and engagement of our students to ensure belonging and full inclusion."

When Joshua was hired, in the seventh year of the strategic plan, his job description dictated that he fulfill it. Larger projects, completing the construction of a new humanities building and concluding the capital campaign, took precedence without a doubt. But as a new leader he did not want to shortchange other aspects of the strategic plan. Joshua understood the significance of the goal of educational identity and its desired outcomes. This was one of the key factors that attracted him to this school. He saw it as a core competency of the school and welcomed this opportunity to lean into it.

He focused on the objective of creating the full-time position for student life and engagement, developing a job description that focused on cultivating an environment for students where all would feel affirmed and included, through programming and resources. He could also tell that it was a source of some contention, as some thought it an unnecessary objective. Why do we need to appoint an individual to assume the responsibility for something we already do? Yet, when Joshua would ask in what ways this is being lived out and made apparent, it was so difficult to articulate: it's something you can feel when you come on campus . . . it's in our community . . . it's a marinade that we are immersed in . . . it is a thread that is woven into the fabric of who we are . . . our kids are so nice and kind, what else would they be but welcoming?

The solution seemed clear, at least in this sense. Appoint an expert with knowledge of how to do this and initiate some obvious, relevant, and large gesture that reflects the ideals. Hence the birth of the first all-school assembly, which had as its mission to encapsulate the theme of inclusivity and appreciation of the richness of differences and diversity in our community. Simple and poised to punctuate the already embraced ideals of the school identity, it seemed a straight-forward, technical fix to an underestimating, profound, and adaptive challenge.

The DIGNITY Lens

YIELD
What do we want our efforts to yield? And how do we know if we've reached our goals?

DIVERSITY
Who is here and who is missing? Assess, interrogate, and leverage the diversity in the community. Dignity connects us regardless of our differences.

TRANSPARENCY
What is our story and how do we tell it? Know the purpose. Tell the story.

IDENTITY
Who are we? Our identity is our anchor. It drives our purpose, our work.

INTEGRITY
Are we doing what we say we are doing? Are our actions aligned with our identity?

GROWTH
Are we willing to grow in some new competencies? Reflect, imagine new ways of being, be open to learning, and choose growth.

NURTURE
What new behaviors do we need to make? Become imagineers. Create an environment of experimentation and innovation.

THE STORY THROUGH
THE DIGNITY LENS

A dream doesn't become reality through magic; it takes sweat, determination, and hard work.

—*Colin Powell*

Let's look again at this story. The goal was clear, the strategy, seemingly simple, and yet, the result was explosive:

Aspiration: To foster an inclusive and healthy learning environment that recognizes and affirms the unique abilities and stories of each individual so that each may realize their full potential.

Strategy: To hire a student life and engagement expert who will, by creating an all-school assembly and other means of engagement, seek to highlight the theme of inclusivity and an appreciation of the richness of differences and diversity in the community.

Reality: A surprising and viscerally divisive response of confusion, suspicion, and misunderstanding from the community.

What does this tell us? The strategy chosen did produce some progress towards the educational identity goal but deeper, more difficult challenges that also needed to be addressed were left unanswered. This was not a technical challenge, one that could easily be solved by hiring an expert or performing a large gesture, like an all-school assembly, without adequate forethought. This challenge lives in a different realm, where people's dignity resides—from Jehan, the faultless and excited teenager, to Derek, the teacher who felt ill equipped, to the disgruntled parent, confused and blindsided, to the school leadership, blissfully unaware of the brewing explosion. This dignity challenge typically surfaces when communities endeavor to become more authentic, by closing the gap between who we want to be and who we currently are. Why? Because to narrow the gap means taking up new behaviors, unmooring from what is comfortable and familiar, shifting perspectives, and mobilizing folks who are reticent to join in the work. The DIGNITY lens provides a comprehensive, holistic, and reflective set of strategies to help achieve the aspiration, the dream. Not by magic at all, but by determined, intentional, and hard work.

Let's look again at this story through the seven strategies of the DIGNITY lens. Each strategy identifies new competencies that require increased capacity by individuals and systems to achieve authentic community. Because the strategies are not linear, we can enter the story through any one of them. They are interrelated and do build on each other but, like a merry-go-round, you can hop on at any time. Ultimately, however, to be successful and attain the hoped-for results, all seven strategies must be engaged. For the purposes of this conversation and for a clear outline, we will look at the story using each strategy as it appears in the order of the word DIGNITY.

PART 2

THE DIGNITY LENS: SEVEN STRATEGIES

DIGNITY

DIVERSITY

People don't learn by staring into a mirror; people learn by encountering difference.

—*Ron Heifetz*

Who is here and who is missing?

Assess, interrogate, reconcile, and leverage the diversity in the community.

Dignity connects us regardless of our differences.

The Story: *Who exactly makes up our student body and wider school community? Is there an opportunity to further lean into this educational identity by being intentional about who comprises our community? For this all-school assembly we decided to illuminate the diversity in our religious representations at this school. But did we assess the climate at our school regarding religious differences? Did we get a sense of the capacity of our community to embrace and appreciate different religious expressions? Does the school community understand why this is even important? Was it enough to rely solely on the director of student life and engagement? Who else in the community could have been invited into this conversation?*

The D in DIGNITY refers to the universality of human diversity. To respect the dignity of all human beings means understanding and recognizing the individual differences and experiences each possess. But wait—before we continue, let us take some time here to re-spect (look again at) the meaning of the word "diversity." I imagine that if you were to ask five people to define "diversity" you might get ten different responses. The word has become laden with a range of values, understandings, and interpretations. Sometimes emotions, personal experiences, or simply a lack of understanding or connection to the term influence its meaning and authentic embrace. Despite being hijacked by multiple interpretations and perhaps even misinformed projections, its definition is simple. It refers to differences. Humanity is inherently diverse, regarding many aspects of our physicality, our brain functioning and learning styles, and so much more, and despite the unfortunate manifestations of inequality, racism, sexism, ageism, and many other "isms" that influence sociopolitical, economic, and legal systems, all human beings are born free and equal in dignity and rights. Each person brings something unique and different to our communal existence. We each have our own journeys, our own stories, and our own experiences. To describe a community, a group, an organization, a gathering, as diverse is simply stating a fact. Diversity refers to difference. That is all. No political agenda. No moral imperative. Just difference.

While diversity is inherent to our humanity, we cannot assume it will be valued. Rather, it is incumbent on us, wherever we find ourselves, to create a climate where difference is recognized, respected, and leveraged and where community members feel fully engaged, confident, and empowered to present their full selves, their best selves and their most productive selves. As a tenet in DIGNITY, this strategy questions how to leverage difference to maximize engagement and productivity and to attain new levels of innovation, learning, and problem-solving. It develops a core competency for any community to thrive. This strategy consists of four action items: to assess, interrogate, reconcile, and leverage diversity in community.

Assess

To assess the diversity in your community, begin by asking who is present and who is missing. Consider the makeup of your community as it is. Who do you see? Who don't you see? What voices are being heard? What voices are silenced? In the case of this school, what religions are present? Which ones aren't? The same questions go for race, socioeconomic background, family structure or family of origin, and geography, among many other differentiators. What about students with different learning styles, or coming from different educational backgrounds such as home-schooling or other non-traditional educational models? What is important is determining who is in the proverbial room and who we may benefit from including. What cognitive skills or experiential skills may contribute to the growth and efficacy of our communities? "The engagement and empowerment of an increasingly diverse talent pool is the highly urgent imperative. Inclusion truly impacts the bottom line through increased employee engagement, productivity, innovation, and retention."[1]

There are many comprehensive assessment instruments with which to do this—comprehensive and narrative surveys, self-reporting tools or dashboards. These tools deliver tangible results

---

1. Shirley Engelmeier, *Inclusion: The New Competitive Business Advantage* (Minneapolis: InclusionINC Media, 2012), book synopsis.

that help shape the strategy for building and sustaining the diversity needed in the system. These tools can also help to assess attitudes, assumptions, beliefs, expectations, and understandings in the community. The purpose is to increase the capacity in the system for embracing diversity in new ways, not necessarily to change people's minds. A formal assessment is very helpful but may not always be necessary, especially depending on the size of our community. What about simply talking to the people around us to get a sense of the different stories present? Creating spaces and opportunities for our colleagues to share their stories is important. It builds an atmosphere of affirmation, inclusion, openness, and trust. This first strategic step may include having in-depth interviews or open conversations, where people feel encouraged to share their full selves without fear of repercussions. This type of open communication is only possible in an environment that says it is acceptable to be your authentic self in this space. But creating welcoming spaces to bring one's whole self does not mean putting identifiers on display. It means including and appreciating and seeing with a new lens.

Let us revisit Jehan's invitation to be a part of this all-school assembly. Her Muslim faith is what distinguished her and what was invited to be embraced and celebrated. It was her faith rather than her personhood that was on display here. From her perspective, Jehan was thrilled to share a part of her story. Thrilled that a space had been created to bring her whole self. The explosive response to her doing that, however, showed the potentially grave danger in a limited focus on cultural identifiers in isolation. Somehow in that instance, Jehan was no longer seen as Jehan, but rather, a practicing Muslim. To respect every human being requires us truly to see others, lest we either become perpetrators of or victims of what Ralph Ellison aptly captured when he said, "I am invisible . . . people refuse to see me . . . they see only my surroundings, themselves or figments of their imagination . . . everything and anything except me."[2] That is why the DIGNITY lens is crucial. With intentionality and deliberateness, we can adjust our lens and see beyond.

And this is not relegated to interpersonal interaction; the danger is also possible in whole communities and societies. Francis Fukuyama in his insightful and timely book on identity, shifts the geopolitical conversations by focusing on the demand for dignity. "The rise of identity politics in modern liberal democracies is one of the chief threats that they face, and unless we can work our way back to more universal understandings of human dignity, we will doom ourselves to continuing conflict."[3] The DIGNITY lens invites us to view the richness of diversity through the lens of human dignity, rather than the more familiar lens of identifiers such as ability, age, ethnicity, gender, race, religion, sexual orientation, socioeconomic status, body image, educational background, academic/social achievement, family of origin or family make-up, geographic or regional background, citizen or migrant status, language, learning style, beliefs (political social, religious), and globalism or internationalism.[4] Yes, in the assessment, numbers and percentages are helpful for clarity and accurate accounting. They are grounding and hold us accountable as the Yield strategy will expound on. But numbers can be restricting. There is risk in defining human beings by numbers and their corresponding demographic and cultural identifiers. It

---

2. Ralph Ellison, *Invisible Man* (New York: Random House, 1994), 3.

3. Fukuyama, *Identity*, 42.

4. "Sample Cultural Identifiers," National Association of Independent Schools, accessed March 4, 2020, *https://www.nais.org/articles/pages/sample-cultural-identifiers. aspx.*

can taint what we see and how we see. DIGNITY expands the limitations of diversity. Instead of constructing discrete lines of identifiers, setting up an "us and them" dynamic, it allows for new partnerships, shared experiences, increased understanding and genuine appreciation.

Interrogate

After assessing the diversity in our community and identifying just who is and who is not present, we then must interrogate why. It is not enough to say that we are missing certain people who may bring new identities, different skills and experiences and different stories to bear. We then need to ask why they are missing. Is there an intentionality behind these choices? Are we intending to exclude some people and include others? If it is not intentional, then what reasons have contributed to their presence or absence? These questions are not about assigning blame or guilt. Asking these questions helps to surface patterns, either of avoidance or perpetuation of tradition, history, or simply familiarity and comfort. Perhaps they are also patterns of fear, which often block the ability to see new meaning in the very thing you're afraid of. In Jehan's school, where respecting and embracing differences is understood to be entrenched in the educational identity, why couldn't the community embrace this part of her? Why was there such a visceral response to her reading from the Quran? It is necessary for the school to assess just what stories are already present in their community, to consider what stories are missing and to understand why they're missing. The reflective and in-depth interrogation may surface unflattering realities, which we are not meant to be ashamed of. On the contrary, we learn from them and decide how and when to pivot. Delving into these questions helps provide the groundwork for developing steps towards reconciling the gaps in the system.

Reconcile

What happens next? Our identity and purpose are integral to the reconciliation process. Who are we and what is our purpose? What is our work and who do we need to accomplish it? What forms of diversity would impact our community's effectiveness and can we create a plan to achieve that diversity? Does Joshua's school need other students of differing faith backgrounds? What about faculty members who are of different faiths? And in our specific contexts? What do we need? Youth, gender diversity, urban vs. rural perspectives? Perhaps we need legal expertise or people with finance or entrepreneurial experience. Whatever it is, be thoughtful and remain tethered to the mission, identity, and purpose of the community. I do recognize this type of change and growth does not occur overnight. But it does take intentionality and focus in myriad avenues such as hiring practices, admission practices, outreach, marketing and communication, and establishing strategic partnerships. Who do we invite? Simultaneously, we need to ensure that our communities, even if they are not yet reflecting the type of diversity that aligns with our work and purpose, cultivate an awareness, acknowledgement, and appreciation of difference. Pay attention to the cultivation of a climate of openness and inclusion.

What does that look like? First, use the results from the assessment tools to get a sense of the current collective understanding of diversity in the system. The tenets in DIGNITY work together. Not in succession from one to the next, but in concert with each other. We cannot create an environment that *nurtures* the diversity in our community without first *assessing* the diversity and determining the needs. Ascertain where the gaps are and what the needs are in the community. This insight about the climate of the community should be given focused consideration before investing human capital in any new efforts. We need to know this information in order to mobilize a shared commitment to this work. Acknowledge the challenges, the difficulties, the areas for growth. Audit what we are already doing to further these efforts. What do we have in place that promotes or builds awareness around affirmation of difference and inclusion? Benchmark with like communities. How do we compare? Are there best practices that we need to familiarize ourselves with? Or professional development or training opportunities that may be needed to acquire new knowledge, skill, and acumen?

Leverage

The need for diversity is no longer couched as a moral or political imperative. It is a core competency, a business strategy, a reality that is integral to the success and flourishing of any community. Former attorney general of the United States Eric Holder says it this way: "I can't actually imagine a time in which the need for diversity will ever cease."[5] Being globally aware and working across difference helps us to make more informed decisions and acquires "transferable skills that will be useful to [us] and will remain with [us] for life."[6] The global economy is evolving such that increasingly organizations need to know how best to work

---

5. World Leaders Forum, February 23, 2012, Columbia University.

6. José Picardo, "Why Students Need a Global Awareness and Understanding of Other Cultures," *The Guardian*, September 25, 2012, http://www.theguardian.com/teacher-network/2012/sep/25/students-global-awareness-other-cultures.

with diverse markets. A diverse collection of skills and experiences (for example, languages, cultural understanding, etc.) allows organizations to reach a wider global audience.[7] The evidence is compelling. A diverse inclusive environment results in multiple benefits for our communities.

We need to consider the ways in which our specific communities can leverage the benefits of the diversity among us. Harness the differences in the room to generate collaboration and creative problem-solving. Be open. Listen. Solicit multiple perspectives to tackle difficult challenges. Innovation is best attained through cognitive diversity or diversity of thought. Embrace different ways of thinking, work collaboratively across groups. Invite others into the work. We learn when we encounter difference. DIGNITY develops the courage to be comfortable being uncomfortable by reminding us that our dignity connects us regardless of our differences.

---

7. Josh Greenberg, "Diversity in the Workplace: Benefits, Challenges and Solutions," accessed March 4, 2020, *https://easysmallbusinesshr.com/2010/08/diversity-in-the-workplace-benefits-challenges-and-solutions/*.

DIGNITY

IDENTITY

. . . I want to remind us that during moments of transition, during moments of tension, it is important to affirm our core identity.

—Bishop Michael Curry

Make your work to be in keeping with your purpose.

—Leonardo da Vinci

> Who are we? Our identity is our anchor. It drives our purpose, our work.
>
> Define. Reiterate and implement your identity.

The Story: *What is the educational identity of the school? "A school that fosters an inclusive and healthy learning environment where the unique abilities and stories of each student are recognized and affirmed so that each may reach their full potential." This value drives our purpose as an educational institution. How has educational identity been lived out in previous years and in what new ways is it being lived out now? Have we done an identity audit? Have we looked back and understood the founding DNA? Do we understand why this was* *important then and why it is of value now, and how it is influenced by current realities? Do we know our areas of strength, our vulnerabilities, and our triggers as a system when it comes to our identity? Where have we lived well into this identity and what are the areas of improvement and growth? Can we look back and see the most unflattering parts of our history when it comes to this identity and purpose, own them, address them, and pivot to a new direction? How has this been articulated before? Have we defined for ourselves and our community—our faculty and staff, students, and parents—what this identity actually means, in terms of our mission, our vision and aspiration, our history?*

Without a clear sense of identity, DIGNITY work will not flourish. Our identity anchors our work and drives our purpose and direction. Identity lies at the root of the dream, of the aspiration. It shapes where we want to go and what we want to be. Too often, we let it sit and atrophy, only referring to it when it is convenient or as a punctuation to some change. Identity in DIGNITY is not static. It cannot sit silent and crystallize into sweet sentimentality. In DIGNITY, identity has energy and life and steers the work. Identity is the wind that whips up the tornado of imagination and creativity. It is also our mirror as we strive for authenticity. Everything that we do, all that we produce, the values we uphold, the dream we aspire to, all hinge on our identity and purpose both individually and in community. Not only that, a firm, collective commitment to our identity and purpose will counter resistance to dignity work and to any change in general. Hugh O'Doherty, expert in developing adaptive leadership capacity from Cambridge Leadership Associates and Harvard Kennedy School of Government, expounds on the centrality of identity and purpose by delineating its crucial features:

"[An] orienting anchor, [it] allows you to hold steady in the face of resistance, [it] prevents you from being guided only by passion; staying connected to purpose allows us to manage egotistic hungers for recognition, power etc., and a shared purpose provides the energy and momentum for the journey . . . to endure discomfort to attain something meaningful."[1] This identity strategy in DIGNITY asks us to conduct an "identity audit" and has at its core three main objectives: to define, maintain, and live out our identity in all that we do.

Define

"What is our identity?" First, let's look to our founding DNA, for that is where the aspirational identity began. What is the original reason for which we were created? Or, if this is the beginning of a new community, who do we want to be? For what purpose? Do the work necessary to define the reason for being. Interwoven in this identity are our values. What do we value? What are our non-negotiables? We orient community around the stated identity. In the Story, the school aimed to reclaim their identity in their strategic plan, and orienting the community around the meaning and value of that identity was key. Had they conducted a sufficient "identity audit," gaining knowledge and understanding from their past to inform their identity today? Sometimes we may have inherited an identity that needs to be refined or redefined or reclaimed. That is why it is important to look to the founding DNA: if it is a collective determination and decision to move away from the original purpose, knowing and understanding the

---

1. Hugh O'Doherty, "Leadership and Purpose," Clergy Leadership Project, Class XXV, Trinity Episcopal Retreat Center, West Cornwall, Connecticut, 2005.

context in which the community was formed is crucial in order to pivot. It is possible to shift away from even the most unflattering interpretation of the original purpose. Just know that what you discover in the founding also informs your present identity. The beauty of using the DIGNITY lens is to see the vast potential for change. It is not seeing what is, but rather, what can be and making an intentional choice about aligning to a new identity. Whether the identity is old, new, or has been refashioned, it remains the basis of our aspiration. It is the foundation of our dream. Know it and make it known. Build consensus around it. Name it. Say it. Be it.

Maintaining the Dream-Identity

It is not enough to claim an identity and then not refer to it regularly. There is danger in losing sight of our identity and settling back into the status quo. There is also danger in proclaiming it intermittently or only in response to a problem or some resistance. This is the very definition of deferred maintenance. DIGNITY relies on the intentional and consistent maintenance of identity. Without that, any progress towards authenticity is limited if not stunted. The word itself is instructive as its Latin root, *identidem*, actually means "repeatedly, again and again." Reiterating in multiple ways, through multiple avenues. We must continue to reiterate our communal identity so it can permeate the community and become a shared purpose. Individuals can then acclimatize or simply discover their work in maintaining the dream-identity. The shared purpose empowers and emboldens creativity, innovation, adaptability, and problem-solving to iterate on the common identity in the face of resistance or change.

The world is constantly changing and affecting the way we see ourselves and how we are seen by others. Without attention to the dream-identity, there is great possibility for inauthenticity and even demise. Langston Hughes's, in his poem "Harlem," eloquently reveals the potential dangers of deferring the maintenance of the dream-identity. I used this poem in a presentation at the National Association of Episcopal Schools Biennial 2018, to illuminate the essential work of maintaining Episcopal identity in Episcopal schools in the face of a changing world. It is a helpful paradigm when reflecting upon the efficacy of any organization or institution. The poem begins with an insightful question, one we must consider in our work toward authentic community: What happens to a dream deferred?

> What happens to a dream deferred?
> Does it dry up
> like a raisin in the sun?
> Or fester like a sore—
> And then run?
> Does it stink like rotten meat?
> Or crust and sugar over—
> like a syrupy sweet?
> Maybe it just sags
> like a heavy load.
>
> *Or does it explode?*[2]

For our purposes, the dream is the identity that drives the purpose. The challenges vary depending on the context, but can

---

2. Langston Hughes, "Harlem," *Selected Poems of Langston Hughes* (New York: Random House, 1959), 268. Originally published in *Montage of a Dream Deferred*, 1951.

include political climate, cultural shifts, economic pressures, competing demands, increased competition, and so on. Certainly, in the Story, the rising tension around Muslims and their faith in the news, and the recent travel ban contributed significantly to the explosive reactions to Jehan reading from the Quran in the all-school assembly. The possible results of deferred maintenance range from crusting over like a syrupy sweet, crystallizing into an adorned statue of lost potential to the dream-identity sagging like a heavy load. Becoming a burden. Something that is omnipresent but we no longer know what to do with it. It is a struggle to explain or describe. It is something that is central but difficult to manage. It is the proverbial elephant in the room. A strong sense of identity may be something we admire in others and even aspire to for ourselves and our various communities, but it can be easier to skirt the issue than to face the conversation head on. Or maybe it explodes, as it did in the opening Story, when a seemingly innocent action resulted in a quagmire of emotions, divisiveness, and suspicion. Is the deferred dream-identity always a ticking time bomb? Will it have explosive consequences if not tended to and nurtured? The good news about this DIGNITY lens is that even if there are explosive consequences or other outcomes that don't move participants toward narrowing the gap between aspiration and reality, there is always room to learn and try again. In DIGNITY, there is never failure. Even the worst moment is not the defining moment, only an opportunity for learning and adaptability. There is infinite potential to pivot and try again.

Live Out the Identity

This is the action part. The tending to and nurturing the identity part. This is where the identity moves from static to dynamic.

From aspiration to action. From ideal to ideas. The strategy behind this tenant of DIGNITY is the conscious and informed work of looking at all proposed actions through the lens of the identity. How does this new initiative advance our collective identity? Why are we going in this direction? Does it align with our identity? What is the relationship between the path being considered and our identity? Does it challenge identity and if so, how and for what purpose? How can we connect with others around a shared identity? How can we support others? How do we stay alive, remain enlivened by the identity, even in the face of opposition? Identity is not a punctuation to the work. Rather, it must inform and steer the strategic work.

One More Thing . . . The "I" of Identity

Notice that this identity work does not come from any one part of the community. Not the leadership alone. Not the "expert." Not the authority. In this work, we all play a role. It is a shared responsibility and obligation oriented around a shared identity and purpose. Does "the way we've always done it" reflect/enliven/embrace/connect to our identity? Are we willing to iterate? Are we willing to thoughtfully experiment within the parameters of the identity and shared purpose? There is always an "I" in identity: the self, and the role each person plays and how we manage ourselves in the midst of this work. Be self-reflective. What is my story? How am I embracing this identity? Do I connect to the identity? What work can I take up to bolster the identity? What are my own strengths and my vulnerabilities? What is my level of comfort in this work? Am I able to partner in this work even if I am uncomfortable and out of my comfort zone? Am I able to see the larger purpose and meaning in the dream-identity?

Am I willing to orient my work and attitude to achieve that? Essentially, if I do connect with this identity, then I am presented with a challenge. Either I need to proactively raise concerns about our direction and provide suggestions to nuance the identity, or see the potential in the dream-identity and seek further understanding and widen my comfort zone, or decide that I cannot get on board with this aspiration and choose to be elsewhere. We all play a part in creating authenticity in our work environments, and it takes courage and a choice to discern how we do that, which brings us to another strategy in DIGNITY, growth.

DIGNITY

GROWTH

The strongest principle of growth lies in the human choice.

—*George Eliot*

> Are we willing to grow in some new competencies?
>
> Reflect, imagine new ways of being, be open to learning, choose growth.

The Story: *What new understanding can we gain here? In what ways do we need to grow? How do we equip our community—our students, our parents, our faculty and staff—with the tools to increase their capacity to imagine new understandings and new ways of being? How do we listen and affirm the disgruntled voices while gently reminding them of the educational identity we espouse? How do we become vulnerable enough to hear those unflattering and perhaps even misconstrued interpretations of our actions? How do we acknowledge emotional responses without sacrificing the progress we are striving for in attainment of the aspirational identity?*

IGNITY work at its core invites us to grow, to progress from our present reality towards our aspirational identity. In DIGNITY, growth is not a given, it is a choice and it is not easy. DIGNITY work requires the self-reflective, uncomfortable work of being present to what we think we know, looking again, and unearthing new ways of seeing and being. That requires considerable growth, personally and together as a whole. Fortunately, if we see ourselves through a DIGNITY lens, if we respect our own dignity, we see immense capacity and ample opportunity to choose growth. Growth is not about getting it right all the time, nor is it necessarily about fundamentally changing who we are. It is about recognizing who we are, leveraging our own gifts and talents, and adopting an openness to learning, leaning into discomfort and developing new competencies. In DIGNITY, growth, unlike change, has one direction and that direction veers towards authenticity. We grow into and out of our authentic selves. Our communities also then become more authentic, as we grow and transform into the very persons and groups of integrity we profess to be. DIGNITY work implies that the results will take time. There is no immediate solution, only striving towards the ultimate goal. That striving invites us to grow in courage, capacity, comprehension, and candor.

Growth in Courage

It takes courage to see ourselves and others with new eyes. It takes courage to look through a DIGNITY lens at ourselves and others, and through the DIGNITY lens at the work to be done. It takes courage to be reflective, seeing both our strengths and our vulnerabilities. It takes courage to take up new behaviors, and even to imagine new possibilities. DIGNITY work is uncomfortable but, oh, so necessary. It takes courage to be a partner in the larger work of a community. It may indeed be easier to defer the work to others who appear to have more expertise or authority in a particular area, but each one of us needs to choose to be a part of the work even if it is unfamiliar and we feel less competent. In the Story, the work to foster a diverse learning environment was placed solely in the hands of Sofia and in her role as the director of student life and engagement. Similarly, in many independent schools, inclusion and equity work is often relegated to directors of diversity or officers of equity and inclusion. But that "human dignity" work, which transcends classrooms and special assemblies and theatrical performances and athletic games, business and communications offices, before, during and after school, belongs to all in the community. DIGNITY shifts the responsibility of growth work from one expert to all involved. And that is why it is difficult work. It takes courage and intentionality to shift our work beyond our immediate tasks to consider the challenging aspects of DIGNITY work. As John F. Kennedy once said, "Effort and courage are not enough without purpose and direction."[1] The courage to grow is inextricably linked to the shared purpose, the dream-identity.

Courage in DIGNITY looks like curiosity—asking questions and being willing to learn and develop new competencies. It is the courage to question our own assumptions, narratives, biases, stereotypes, and understandings in light of a larger purpose. It is positioning ourselves to seek out creative and innovative solutions and challenge the status quo. It is in the necessary difficult conversations, as disruptive and challenging as they may be. It is

---

1. Remarks at Reynolds Coliseum, Raleigh, NC, September 17, 1960, *https://www.jfklibrary.org/archives/other-resources/john-f-kennedy-speeches/raleigh-nc-19600917*.

the ability to be comfortable being uncomfortable. It is owning our "stuff," persistently working with it for the good. This courage does not lead to "Kumbayah" moments when everyone gets along. Rather it creates a climate in which we are not averse to conflict, where reconciliation is possible and viable, partnerships more readily attainable, and growth and transformation more sustainable.

Growth in Capacity

What is the capacity in the community for this type of growth? What can the community sustain in terms of growth and transformation? DIGNITY enables us to stretch and develop our capacity. There is always room for growth and transformation, even extraordinary transformation. However, as George Eliot so astutely captured it, the principle behind this capacity to grow is rooted in human choice, and the choices we make in DIGNITY should point us towards closing the gap between who we say we are and our lived reality. "We must make the choices that enable us to fulfill the deepest capacities of our real selves."[2] Our willingness to adapt, to try on something new, and simultaneously our willingness to accept loss, especially of the familiar, increases our capacity.

What is one of the greatest obstacles to true growth? Clinging to the familiar or "we've always done it this way." The disgruntled parents who voiced their resentment of including a reading from the Quran in the assembly were grieving what was familiar. It required an increased capacity on their part to see a different interpretation of the event. The teacher, Derek, too, had to learn

---

2. Thomas Merton, *No Man Is an Island* (New York: Harcourt, Inc., 1955), 25.

new competencies to manage his students' rising emotions and facilitate a thoughtful and purposeful conversation. According to Marty Linsky from the Kennedy School of Government at Harvard University, no one is afraid of change per se. What we fear, he contends, is the loss that comes with change.[3] Yes, there will be loss. As we choose to take up new behaviors, we must let some old behaviors go and we will need to somehow grieve that loss as we accept it, especially as it moves us closer to the dream-identity. DIGNITY invites us to increase our capacity to imagine new possibilities. When we engage in this work we are able to envision different perspectives and create a more holistic picture of the larger purpose. The DIGNITY lens enables us to see possibility growing out of loss, to see progress instead of problems, and to see hope instead of despair.[4]

Growth in Comprehension

How we grow depends on our openness to learn and understand. DIGNITY work thrives if the expectation of learning is clearly articulated. As a college professor I loved the "aha" moments in the classroom, the striving to understand a topic from multiple perspectives. There is dignity in the multiple ways individuals have come to understand the same topic. The diversity of thought is vast and expansive and, frankly, is worthy of being heard and understood. All thoughts matter! We may not agree with everything but anticipating a breadth of points of view and interpretations only better prepares us for adhering to the choices we make, as we face resistance and conflict. Knowing this gives us

---

3. O'Malley and Cebula, *Your Leadership Edge*, 134.
4. Ibid.

the power and authority and freedom to listen to others, strive for empathy, be open to new ideas, collaborate with others, and create an atmosphere where all feel safe to share their ideas and be heard. It is important to clarify that the invitation to share ideas and to listen actively to others is not an invitation to be solely reactionary: it is an invitation to be thoughtful and purposeful in presenting ideas. This intentionality centers around the ability to reflect on the way you think and present evidence for your ideas, rather than simply relying on personal reasoning and emotion as sufficient proof. The Yield strategy of DIGNITY focuses on the importance for evidence-based learning and insight.

Growth in Candor

Working with others in the context of transformation and growth has the potential to illicit emotional reactions and responses. Sometimes they may be even visceral and heated. This is not unexpected when it comes to letting go of deeply held values and beliefs of the familiar, of what is known and what is comfortable. To mitigate this, there is an elegance and control in how we listen and express our ideas in DIGNITY work, best described as "kind candor." Candor is simply the ability to be honest, sincere, and authentic in expression. Kind candor is the ability to give voice to disagreement, to listen to tough experiences, and to have difficult conversations without violating the dignity of others. When parents such as Susan approached Joshua, the school leader, following the assembly with their anger and confusion and even misconstrued conclusions, he had to maintain a level of curiosity rather than defensiveness to deflate the emotion. He had to actively listen and not avoid the unease of hearing criticism or accusations about the school's intentions. Listening also means being able to use the criticism as insight and information about the capacity of the community and then how to adjust going forward. He had to be a good steward of that information. Additionally, his adherence to the identity of the school and consistent redirection to that being the ultimate driver of new initiatives such as this assembly enabled him to respond with kind candor and to remain steady in the midst of the hurricane of emotions. Candor is possible when we are present to the assumptions, beliefs, conjectures, theories, and notions that color what we see and still remain curious. It is not easy. It is possible.

DIGNITY

NURTURE

Always be on the lookout for ways to nurture your dream.

—*Laozi*

What new behaviors do we need to make? Become imagineers.

Create an environment of experimentation and innovation.

The Story: *What have we put in place to nurture our educational identity? If we are to foster and cultivate an inclusive and healthy learning environment where the unique abilities and stories of each individual are recognized and affirmed so that each may realize their full potential, what initiatives have been implemented to reflect and nourish this ideal? What have we created—for our parents, our students, our faculty and staff—to foster an environment that values dialogue and understanding about differences? What programming is available for our community to encourage a sense of belonging in this community? How have we communicated that sharing all parts of ourselves is welcomed and valued? How have we engaged our business office, our student life team, our counseling team, our college counseling team, our enrollment management and admissions* *team, our curriculum planning team to further advance the educational identity?*

Dream-identities will wither like raisins in the sun if we fail to do the things we must do to make them come to fruition. To always seek ways to nurture the dream means to have an audacious imagination. The world of reality has its limits, but the world of imagination is boundless.[1] This is the strategic inspiration behind "nurture" in DIGNITY. It creates a community of "imagineers,"[2] with just the right balance of wild imagination and thoughtful, skilled engineering. The imagineering work in DIGNITY is based on experimentation; we cannot know the outcome, we only know we are making a strategic choice to get us closer to the dream realized. But experiments are not based on feelings and knee-jerk reactions. They are deliberate, strategic choices made to move us closer to the dream-identity. While they carry with them the uncertainty and discomfort of the unknown, what is the alternative? The frustration of a dream never realized? The consequences of a dream deferred? There is no need for fear or hesitation in experimenting, because there is no failure in DIGNITY, only learning. The DIGNITY lens emboldens us to take up these new behaviors without the fear of missing the mark. If our ultimate goal is to be an authentic community, where what we say and who we are align, then each experiment, no matter the outcome, is another opportunity to nurture the dream. As we do so, we must create a climate of experimentation, be aware of the pace at which we experiment, and know how to manage the anxiety that comes along with it.

---

1. Jean-Jacques Rousseau, *Emile Ou De L'Education (Emile, or Treatise on Education)* 1762.

2. While the term "imagineering" is associated with Walt Disney Imagineering Research and Development, Inc., the creative force behind memorable Disney experiences that was founded in 1952 by Walt Disney, it is used here purely as a creative merging of words.

Climate of Experimentation

"Power to the imagination! Be realistic. Demand the impossible." Angela Davis has used these slogans[3] from the 1960s to point to the power of imagination in radically transforming our current realities. Theologian Walter Brueggemann also refers to the use of imagination, the prophetic imagination, when proposing alternative futures: "[Q]uestions of implementation are of no consequence until the vision can be imagined. The imagination must come before the implementation."[4] So what do we need to keep the dream alive? What do we need to nurture the dream? Imagine the wildest possibilities. Go there first. Consider the boundless possibilities and then consider the practical ways of how to get there. That is the imagineering process—wild imagination and purposeful engineering. There are no consequences in imagining innovative ways to enliven the dream. The school leadership imagined an assembly that would capture their refreshed educational identity. Was this the only way they could have imagined? No, but it was a worthwhile experiment in an attempt to work toward the aspirational identity. While the result was unexpected, they can still learn, use the information, identify some of the gaps in its implementation, pivot, and develop a new experiment. What other wild imaginative experiments could the school implement to cultivate "an inclusive and healthy" learning environment? Who will help nurture the dream?

DIGNITY work mobilizes many groups and requires the ability to collaborate across different and relevant groups. We all need to feel confident, encouraged, and safe to share our ideas

---

3. Occupy Philly rally, People's Plaza, City Hall, Philadelphia, PA, October 28, 2011.

4. Walter Brueggemann, *The Prophetic Imagination*, 2nd ed. (Minneapolis: Augsburg Fortress, 2001), 40.

no matter how different they may seem. While not all ideas will advance the identity, all ideas are worthy of being heard. Who else in the school community could have been invited to imagine new ways to enliven the educational identity? But this sense of worthiness will not flourish without a deep sense of trust. Trust that there will be no violations of dignity. Trust that we will be heard. Trust that our stories matter. Trust that our individual differences will be appreciated and not only tolerated. In *Leading with Dignity*, Donna Hicks affirms the necessity of trustworthiness in several of her ten elements of dignity, from "Recognition: Validat[ing] others for their talents, hard work, thoughtfulness and help" to "Benefit of the Doubt: Treat[ing] people as if they are trustworthy."[5]

Pace the Experimentation

There is an elegant choreography in how and when we introduce these experiments. First of all, sustainable transformation does not happen overnight. It takes time. The extraordinary metamorphosis of a caterpillar into a butterfly can take several months. Yet, as Maya Angelou is credited with saying, we often delight in the beauty of the butterfly but rarely admit the changes it has gone through to achieve that beauty. We need to let go of the desire for immediate gratification, yet maintain an urgency of now. DIGNITY work takes time. It takes sustained effort and experimentation to bridge the gap. Is the community ready for this kind of persistent work? Is the community elastic enough to engage in work with uncertain outcomes? Timing is important. Being aware of the full context, both internally and externally,

---

5. Hicks, *Leading with Dignity*, 16, 17.

may also impact timing. Was it wise to introduce the Quran in the all-school assembly just as the Muslim rhetoric in the political arena and in the public imagination was on the rise? If so, could the school have anticipated polarizing responses? If things change significantly too quickly, something may indeed explode. Similarly, being too cautious about introducing a new experiment may demonstrate a lack of confidence or a lack of commitment to achieving the ideal. Strive for a delicate balance of cautious urgency.

Manage the Anxiety

Ever learned a new dance step? When did you last learn to do something you've never done before? Remember the discomfort? The awkwardness? Even the anxiety in the pit of your stomach about the whole process? But, you did it. You pushed through. You knew there was something bigger, something more important than the immediate moment of uneasiness. There is no doubt that anxiety is produced in this process. It is uncomfortable to learn a new behavior. If we are galvanized around the same purpose to nurture the dream-identity, however, we are more likely to stay the course.

Derek, the teacher in our earlier scenario, is faced with quite a situation! What if Derek's first action, beyond his fear, beyond his nervousness, beyond his initial assumptions about his students' responses, was to pause and assess the temperature in the room, then rely on newly acquired skills to address the emotions he found there? Getting a sense of the climate in our community, even within ourselves, is necessary before implementing new behaviors. Derek knows he has a responsibility to foster critical thinking and a learning environment where students listen to each other, learn from one another, and respect the dignity in each other while expressing their authentic voices and raising areas of disagreement. Are the students ready to do that? Are they equipped with previous experience or educational tools? Is Derek willing to lean into discomfort and manage the learning in the classroom without violating anyone's dignity? Is the classroom environment elastic enough to do this? How will Derek galvanize the students around this vision? Are they willing to join him in bringing this vision to reality? There is much to be learned.

In the DIGNITY context, we must create the ideal climate to nurture intellectual, social, and cultural competencies. Whose work is it? Derek's work is to equip himself with new pedagogical tools such as cultural responsive teaching with "multidimensional, emancipatory, transformative, empowering and validating"[6] attributes and to invite the students on this journey. It is the students' work to choose to partner with the teacher and respect the different voices in the room, to be curious, and to have the courage to channel emotions toward learning and deepened understanding. And how are these responsibilities achieved? Through effective and relevant professional development and by introducing ground rules and effective tools and strategies for high discussion-based classroom etiquette and practice. In addition to introducing experiments, we must also pay attention to the ways in which we can support and guide

---

6. Jennifer Zaccara and Roberto d'Erizans, "Culturally Responsive Pedagogy Requires Culturally Responsive Schools," *Independent School*, National Association of Independent Schools, accessed March 4, 2020, *https://www.nais. org/magazine/independent-teacher/spring-2019/culturally-responsive-pedagogy-requires-culturally-responsive-schools/*.

or nurture the experimentation. A climate of experimentation is comprehensive and multidimensional.

In the previous strategy of Growth, we discussed the experience of loss. In this work, we will have to suspend some of our deeply held values so that others may thrive. This loss can also create great angst, but DIGNITY calls us to face the difficulty in embracing new realities and new ways of seeing the world. To nurture does not mean to allow harm to our souls or to be doormats. It takes great courage and curiosity to identify new behaviors, to mobilize others around those new behaviors, to execute them and even to support those taking on those new behaviors. Yes, there will be anxiety but it is not meant to be harmful or destructive. Rather, it should engender curiosity and be healthful. DIGNITY gives us the framework to face the tough challenges and become comfortable in being uncomfortable.

INTEGRITY

Integrity is choosing courage over comfort; choosing what is right over what is fun, fast or easy; and choosing to practice our values rather than simply professing them.

—*Brené Brown*

> Are we doing what we say we are doing? Are our actions aligned with our identity?

The Story: *How are we holding ourselves accountable to the values and identity we say we uphold? How often do we take the time to stop for an "integrity audit" and examine whether our actions are in line with our identity? What does this visceral response in our community, from our parents and students and faculty, tell us about how we have been living out our identity previously?*

ntegrity is the backbone of authenticity. It is our measuring stick, our barometer. Are we doing what we say we are doing? If the answer to this question of integrity is not yes, there is still work to be done. Integrity, in DIGNITY, is an accurate diagnostic. As we take up agency in innovating or experimenting, we need to pause and take an imaginary flight to hover over our community and conduct an integrity audit. Imagine floating, temporarily suspended in air with DIGNITY glasses, looking over the community. As we look from this vantage point, we can see all of the moving parts in our system. We can see who is contributing to the work and what is the nature of their contribution. We can see if progress is being made towards the stated goals with the innovations we have introduced. As we hover, we ask strategic questions: Is our innovation in line with who we are? Will this new innovation advance our identity? What purpose will it achieve? Is it rooted in emotion or is it thoughtful and bolstered with evidence-based insight? The integrity audit or diagnosis is not meant to reveal failure. Rather it helps to create a reliable pathway for our work, revealing blind spots, unused opportunities, potential minefields, and holds us accountable to the values we profess. It, too, is multidimensional and comprehensive. There are four main attributes in the integrity audit: accountability, embracing contradictions, steadiness, and vulnerability.

Accountability

DIGNITY work is thoughtful and strategic work, and taking responsibility for our actions and being answerable to them is an integral part of our efforts. It is as simple as that. Are we doing what we say we are doing? Our work has, at its core, living out our aspirational identities, our stated goals, our vision. In all that we do, are we furthering that vision? And if we are not, why not? Why do we choose the actions we do? Out of comfort or maintaining the status quo? Is it easy, less troublemaking? The integrity audit is our checks and balance system, to be conducted regularly. These best occur both before and after an experiment has been run. Take the time to hover and conduct the audit, in a staff or board meeting or in a conversation over lunch. Let us hold ourselves accountable to the values we profess.

Embracing Contradictions

Contradictions exist. But they do not take away from our integrity. In fact, there is deepened integrity in being able to name them and approach them with curiosity rather than defensiveness. Joshua, for example, and his leadership team sought to lean into the values the school espoused, creating a diverse learning environment. What they also discovered was that there were other competing values, held by some parents, faculty, and students, that challenged the extent to which they could lean in. They learned that there was a deeply held value about what a diverse learning environment looks like, and it did not include reading from the Quran, even though it comes from one of the Abrahamic faiths. The value is the primacy of Christianity in that space. The value is the relegation of inter-religious dialogue to the classroom and to an intellectual exchange, not as an active expression of a community member's beliefs and life. An integrity audit, if thoughtful and multidimensional, can reveal these contradictions and competing values. We can't avoid them. Instead embrace them and be prepared for them. DIGNITY work includes seeing and giving worth to these competing values and being able to adapt and remain steady in the ultimate pursuit of integrity.

Steadiness

The road to authenticity is not smooth and without disruptions. After all, we are striving to assemble and energize a community made up of individuals with a diversity of experiences all yearning to be recognized and respected, around a common goal of aligning our communal identity-dream with our lived reality. This is not easy work! Not everyone values integrity. Not everyone values authenticity. Not everyone agrees on how we get there. The road will be rocky. In DIGNITY work, we must remain steady in our endeavors. When the disgruntled parents made their position clear, even if Joshua and his team did not agree with their conclusions, they held steady. They did not "take it back" in some emotional response just to appease the parents' emotional reactions. They did not reverse their decision, denying the appropriateness of having Jehan read from the Quran. In fact, they held firm to the innovation as an expression of the school's identity. Yes, experiment. Yes, innovate. And then hold it steady. Remain stable. Remain consistent. Rest assured in the imagineering process. Steadiness is not holding your breath with anxiety to wait for the results. Steadiness is resting in the confidence of DIGNITY work.

Vulnerability

We will not always get this work right. We will not always make progress towards our stated goals. We may run experiments that do not take us where we hope to go. We will run experiments that have explosive reactions. There is no shame in confessing and admitting mistakes. There is no shame in confessing the difficulties in a situation. Be vulnerable as a community. Be willing to acknowledge the blind spots and gaps in the innovation. Be willing to hear and respect criticism and any negative feedback. Joshua and his team kept themselves open to the harsh criticism, listening, as hard as it was, and gathering new information. Being vulnerable is not weak or acquiescing to failure. Being vulnerable is positioning ourselves to be open to learning. In DIGNITY there is always room for new knowledge. Knowing this strengthens our authenticity.

DIGNITY

TRANSPARENCY

Language alone protects us from the scariness of things with no names. Language alone is meditation.

—*Toni Morrison*

> What is our story and how do we tell it? Know the purpose. Tell the story.

The Story: *Have we effectively communicated the educational and mission identity of the school to our community? Did we articulate the connection of the new faculty position "director of student life and engagement" and the genesis of the newly envisioned all-school assembly in terms of our strategic plan? Has the connection to our identity and our purpose been made clear? Did we lay the groundwork to make the community aware of the refreshed focus on our school identity and mission? Why was Joshua's manifesto necessary? What was its purpose? Why wasn't an "identity manifesto" written before?*

We all have stories; even communities have stories. Our stories tell us who we are, where we've come from, and where we are going. Everything we do tells our story. What we produce tells our story. How we produce it also reflects what parts of our narrative are maintained and reproduced. The story of a community is intimately tied to its identity, to its aspirational identity, and to its current lived reality. They give direction to our communities, helping to shape our goals and their achievement. While we do have individual stories that influence our work ethic, our connections to the communities, and our ability to partner with the overarching direction of our communities, DIGNITY is more focused on the institutional story and how that is communicated. Being transparent about our institutional stories is a core component in building authenticity into the system. Our institutional stories may vary—some may be on a trajectory consistent with our aspirational identity, and others may have some questionable or unfortunate parts. We don't hide away from these parts in telling our story. There is great strength in embracing the whole story and in putting language to the story; we can write a new ending. We have the institutional power to create our narratives as we move forward to our aspirational goals. Don't jettison the past. Use it to inform the future. We wouldn't be who we are today without the experiences of the past. Authenticity means embracing all of this—even our worst moments and being willing to be transparent about it. It is acceptable to say as a community that we have made poor choices and are now moving in a new direction. Essentially, there is power in telling our stories with transparency and genuineness. We have the power to educate the community, create enthusiasm and energy around the story, to build awareness of the reality surrounding our communities and to create trust and openness. In DIGNITY, transparency consists of four aspects: tell the story, mobilize the community, know the context, communicate along the way.

Tell the Story

Know the purpose. Tell the story. It's as simple as that. Begin by learning the community's story. In the Identity tenet, there is a lot of work done to excavate the institutional story, identifying the founding DNA and archival trajectory and ultimately molding the purpose. Everything we do as a community tells a story. How we interact with and treat the people we work with tells our story; what we produce tells our story; what we *don't* do tells our story. Transparency is giving language to that story and effectively communicating it out to the community. By giving it language, we take control of the narrative. And that is essential in building authenticity. If Jehan's school had effectively been telling its story, would this innovation have caused such a disruption? Did the school take for granted that its story was known and understood? Don't tarry in giving language to the story. As Toni Morrison insightfully captures, language takes away fear, giving words to those things we don't understand, are uncomfortable with or even don't agree with. Language can control our imaginations. Telling our institutional stories not only educates and informs, but eliminates ambiguity and builds trust. Trust is the currency that enables true partnership in the system.

Mobilize the Community

Telling our stories allows the individuals within our communities to understand the big picture. To get a sense of where we have come from, where we are, and where we are going. Knowing this, all of us then have an opportunity to reflect on that story and to assess whether or not we as individuals can partner with that story. We ask ourselves, "What is my connection to this story? What skills do I have to further this story and to advance the aspiration?" This is where the mobilization happens. Narrative transparency listens and acknowledges people's interpretations, hesitations and concerns about the institutional story. It leverages the diversity of thought that both involves and empowers people. Narrative transparency prioritizes mission and identity over emotions. Narrative transparency does not apologize for the identity, instead it holds firm, it continually learns and pivots, and is always open to creative solutions that advance the dream-identity.

Know the Context

Our communities do not exist in bubbles, isolated from the realities of the world. We are surrounded by shifting political, economic, social, and cultural landscapes. It is imperative to be aware of these external factors. Our institutions—our churches, our schools, our small groups—are only microcosmic reflections of the larger society. Knowing our context translates into being judiciously transparent. That may not sound like "true" transparency. But it is not duplicitous. Instead in DIGNITY, this strategic transparency means being wary of becoming so myopic, so focused on our community, that we miss what's influencing us from outside. Strategic transparency protects us from being blindsided as Joshua and his senior team were at the school. In that instance, Joshua and Sophia and others could have viewed the all-school assembly through the lens of the rising anti-Muslim rhetoric in the media, anticipated several responses, and accommodated for them preemptively: by articulating the need for an interfaith dialogue in the midst of the national conversation, for example, or by sharing the assembly program/bulletin before the event occurred. Their planning could have benefitted from involving other strategic groups in the process. Strategic transparency is most effective when it involves working across groups to garner multiple perspectives in an effort to anticipate multiple responses.

Communicate Along the Way

While committing to transparency does not mean sharing inside or confidential information or all the details of the decision-making process, it does invite us to share the triumphs and opportunities for learning along the way. Keeping the community abreast maintains and even reinforces the trust needed in the system. It creates spaces for open dialogue and dismisses any suspicions or skepticism. Healthy skepticism is natural and expected, but no one can deny a community's commitment to transparency, if adequately followed through. The allegiance to transparency is fully in our hands. We decide how much and how often to communicate. The frequency and quantity is often dictated by the capacity of the community for information. There is fear in revealing too much or ultimately being too vulnerable, by being transparent. Yet vulnerability in DIGNITY is a core value. It is not a reflection of weakness or powerlessness. On the contrary, a community's vulnerability is an acknowledgement and recognition of its own collective dignity and the dignity of others.

DIGNITY

YIELD

The goal is to turn data into information, and information into insight.

—*Carly Fiorina*

> What do we want our efforts to yield? And how do we know if we've reached there?

The Story: *At this school, the desired outcome is articulated in the strategic plan: "Live into our educational identity." By what standard will living into the school's educational identity be measured? What measurements have we used in the past? Have there been adequate measurements of this educational ideal? Is there anything to measure ourselves against? Are there other schools who espouse similar beliefs? How do we measure up? Have we benchmarked? What are some key factors that we should be measuring? Religious identities in our student body? Racial and ethnic identities? Sexual orientation and gender identities? Learning styles? Would simply hiring the expert and executing the events be a sufficient measurement of the articulated goal?*

IGNITY work is useless without asking what the efforts will yield. Being able to measure the work is imperative. Dream-identities and aspirational identities need to be grounded in quantifiable metrics. Yes, metrics! What do we want to achieve? And how are we going to measure it? We need data not only to measure what we hope for, but to inform and guide how we will get there. Data shapes the imagineering work. Data drives the creative problem solving. Data also reflects the progress we make as we implement these solutions. Data provides consistency and opportunities to evolve, reflect, and continually grow. DIGNITY work—becoming a more authentic community, closing the gap between our aspirational and lived identity—does not occur in a vacuum. It cannot reside only in our imaginations and our emotions. It must be tied to outcomes and goals so as to hold ourselves accountable, to measure our progress, and to guide our direction. Dream-identities can be measured, we just need to be able to articulate what the specific indicators will be and how to measure them. The Yield tenet essentially asks three questions: What do we want to yield? How will our goals be measured? What do we already know based on current data?

What Do We Want to Yield?

Dream-identities are beautiful and inspirational, but not enough without data. DIGNITY involves strategic work. And strategy is informed by data. Data is not just information. Data provides insight and acumen. It gives the work meaning, purpose, and direction. Where do we want to go? What do we want the yield or outcome of our efforts to include? What are our desired outcomes? At Joshua's school, there were several opportunities for questions around yield. What did the administration identify that they wanted to generate? A more inclusive, diverse learning environment. By what standards could they measure that? The number of religious identities present in the student body? The breakdown of self-reported racial and ethnic identities in the student body? What about other signifiers of diversity in the student body? Did they set out a timeline with objectives and indicators of progress? And what exactly would reflect a diverse learning community—20 percent? 50 percent? Data amplifies and reinforces DIGNITY work. It is not cold and impersonal as sometimes numbers and data can project. Instead data is insightful and brings dimension and color to the aspirational goals we envision. We must couch our aspirational goals in terms of data. Take the time to isolate what parts of the dream-identity can be measured, the end objectives, and then ask, how?

How Will Our Goals Be Measured?

We need to become comfortable with data and the various tools we can use to measure both quantitative and qualitative results of our work. Dashboards, surveys, assessments, in-depth interviews, and small-group "coffee and conversation" gatherings are all effective means of gathering data. They can provide meaningful information that reflect the progress we make as we work to close the gap. How often we measure ourselves and by what means can depend on our community and how they best respond to various types of data gathering. For example, some communities have a greater capacity for completing surveys than others do. Some love the intimacy of small-group gatherings and conversations. Some will welcome both. We know our communities and can determine the most effective and efficient means of assessment. How we do it and how often is up to our discretion, but doing it is nonnegotiable. Data gathering holds us accountable to the work we do and allows us to revisit and reevaluate the work as we proceed. Simultaneously, it guides the direction in which we will go.

What Do We Already Know Based on Current Data?

Data-driven decision-making is what this part of Yield centers around. It is using data to reveal knowledge about who we are as a community, beyond intuition and emotion and feelings. Data is the counterweight to the deep emotions that DIGNITY work can elicit. It grounds this work. Data guards against biases, locates blind spots, gaps, and unresolved questions and also provides solutions for those questions. Mining data for insight and creative solutions is integral to DIGNITY work. Considering Joshua's school, was there sufficient pre-work done, in terms of data gathering, to better support the new initiatives? What, if anything, could the data have revealed about the community's capacity to have multiple voices of faith in the all-school setting? Had there been other Muslim students at the school prior to this event? Were there voices in the community that were seeking an outlet to be heard?

Many measuring tools could have been implemented to access this type of information, from an original survey to small campus-wide conversations. Sometimes the information could be gleaned from a collaborative effort across key constituents in the community. Simply having a conversation that includes multiple perspectives is data gathering. Identify the sources of information and then mine the information for meaning. It can both reflect past and predict future trends and patterns. It can optimize learning and maximize the efforts towards closing the gap.

For some of us, data can be scary and intimidating. It can push people away instead of bringing them closer to the work at hand. But the use of gathering data is worth so much more than some momentary discomfort. In fact, it is an opportunity for productive discomfort—another occasion to grow in capacity and new competencies. Data is simply information. What we glean from it to drive our decisions is invaluable. At times it may affirm our efforts, and at others it may reveal opportunities for growth or occasions for pivoting in a new direction. In DIGNITY, we use data to gain insight into our communities. We use data to enflesh our stories and inform how we attain the very goals we aspire to. So you must become familiar and fluent with hard, qualitative data, numbers, graphs—what and how people think and experience. Whatever it takes! It is all valuable information. It is all important. It is not to be set aside.

SUMMARY

DIGNITY: Diversity, Identity, Growth, Nurture, Integrity, Transparency, and Yield. Seven strategies to build a more authentic community. Together we looked at the Story, a moment in time of this school community, through the lens of these seven strategies. The DIGNITY strategies provided a framework with which to advance their efforts in becoming a more authentic community. That is, living into the very ideals it set out in its educational identity and school mission and culture. So what happened? What followed? How would the implementation of DIGNITY affect the personalities we've come to know and the work of the school? That actually must reside in our imaginations. The very premise of DIGNITY is about closing gaps, intentional efforts to inch closer to the dream-identity we hold for our communities. It is striving, grounded in a new way of seeing the tough problems and challenges we face, and imagineering solutions to transform our aspirational identities into reality. DIGNITY work takes time, and its results not immediate. In fact, they are evolutionary and characterized by progress and adaptation. The genius of analyzing this Story, and any community's striving toward authenticity through the DIGNITY lens, is that it is first and foremost viewed as having great potential for profound transformational change. Remember, it is being able to look closely at the present we are constructing and see the future we are dreaming. With each new intervention, we learn, we grow, we develop new competencies and capacities and we strengthen our path forward.

What does an authentic community look like? There may be many understandings of what an authentic community looks like, but in this book it is simple. It is a community, an institution, an organization whose aspirational identity, as articulated in its stated mission or purpose or identity, mirrors its lived reality. I believe that institutions would benefit in their bottom line and lived experience of maximizing productivity and engagement by striving toward authenticity. And the DIGNITY lens is one way to get there. Below are two examples of communities who, by radical—sometimes completely unorthodox and bold—choices, strive to maintain the dignity of their constituents while aligning their aspirational goals with their lived reality. The following two examples only offer a sample. Are there contradictions and still gaps to be closed in these communities? Yes. Is there work still to be done to realize complete authenticity? Yes. But do these communities reflect aspects of authenticity? Yes, they do.

Chick-fil-A[1]

Identity: Chick-fil-A founder, Truett Cathy, made the decision to close on Sundays in 1946 when he opened his first restaurant in Hapeville, Georgia. Having worked seven days a week in twenty-four-hour restaurants, Cathy saw the importance of closing on Sundays so that he and his employees could set aside one day to rest and worship if they chose—a practice the company upholds today. "Closing our business on Sunday, the Lord's Day, is our way of honoring God and

---

1. Kate Taylor, "Why Chick-fil-A's Decision to Close on Sundays Is a Brilliant Business Strategy," *Business Insider*, June 2, 2019, *https://www.businessinsider.com/chick-fil-a-closed-on-sunday-business-strategy-2019-6*.

showing our loyalty to Him," Cathy writes in his book *Eat Mor Chikin, Inspire More People*.[2] Even locations in airports and sports stadiums remain closed on Sunday, despite the massive number of travelers and hungry football fans seeking fried chicken sandwiches.

Yield: Chick-fil-A is achieving sales numbers no other chicken chain in the industry can top—and it's doing it with one fewer day of the week to work with. Despite being open for 14 percent fewer days a year than competitors, Chick-fil-A is dominating the fast-food industry. The chain's same-store sales grew by 16.7 percent in 2018, according to Nation's Restaurant News data; internal sales figures shared with Business Insider indicate that same-store sales have been up by more than 16 percent so far in 2019 as well.

Transparency: It is well communicated that Chick-fil-A is closed on Sundays, and this is clearly articulated to its team members as well as the general public as an expectation and a value inextricably tied to its brand identity.

Growth: Occasionally, however, locations will open in emergencies, providing free food to those in need. Chick-fil-A prepared free meals for the thousands of passengers stranded after a power failure halted activity at Hartsfield-Jackson Atlanta International Airport. Similar instances happened following the Orlando Pulse nightclub shooting and when tornadoes hit Texas in 2015.[3]

---

2. Truett Cathy, *Eat Mor Chikin, Inspire More People: Doing Business the Chick-fil-A Way* (Looking Glass Books, 2002), 40.

3. Kate Taylor, "Chick-fil-A Is Always Closed on Sunday—Except in These Rare Inspiring Instances," Business Insider, December 18, 2017, *https://www.businessinsider.com/chick-fil-a-opens-sunday-natural-diasters-emergencies-2017-12*.

Nurture: "Initially people might think, well, they're going to do less sales because they closed one day every week," Kalinowski Equity Research founder Mark Kalinowski told Business Insider. "But, there are a lot of benefits to being closed on Sundays." Giving employees and franchisees (referred to as "operators" at Chick-fil-A) at least one day off a week allows them to relax and return rejuvenated to their jobs, Kalinowski says.[4] Closing on Sunday gives employees a chance to recharge, and it creates a sense of community and scarcity among customers.

U.S. Prison Reform (in Connecticut and Pennsylvania) Inspired by European Prison Systems That Emphasize Personal Dignity[5]

Identity: The prison system in Connecticut is aiming to address the high recidivism rates in the U.S. context especially for young women aged eighteen to twenty-five. It is doing so by creating a prison experience that promotes rehabilitation by mimicking the European emphasis on personal dignity and "focus[ing] on therapy and self-improvement, with the idea that rehabilitation will reduce re-offense."[6]

---

4. Kate Taylor, "Why Chick-fil-A's Decision to Close on Sundays Is a Brilliant Business Strategy," Business Insider, June 2, 2019, *https://www.businessinsider.com/chick-fil-a-closed-on-sunday-business-strategy-2019-6*.

5. Maurice Chammah, "To Help Young Women in Prison, Try Dignity," *New York Times*, October 9, 2018, *https://www.nytimes.com/2018/10/09/opinion/to-help-young-women-in-prison-try-dignity.html?referringSource=articleShare*.

6. Brit McCandless Farmer, "The German Prison Program That Inspired Connecticut," CBS News, March 31, 2019, *https://www.cbsnews.com/news/the-german-prison-program-that-inspired-connecticut-60-minutes/*.

Growth: Inspired by European prison culture to nurture the dignity of its prisoners, some U.S. prisons in Pennsylvania are teaching corrections officers to go beyond their security role and think like therapists, while North Dakota has been giving prisoners keys so they can lock their own doors. In Connecticut, officers are trained to talk to women about their traumas and vulnerabilities. There is an emphasis on planning for a crime-free life after release, applying for jobs, and getting frequent opportunities to interview and write résumés.

Nurture: Scott Semple, who runs the Connecticut state prison system, was "struck by a German prison for young adults, in which men and women were housed in a verdant compound that resembled a liberal arts college. They were given intensive therapy and training in trades like welding and farming."[7]

Yield: The recidivism rate in the German prison system is half that of the United States. Semple created a program in June 2018 at the York Correctional Institution, a women's prison in eastern Connecticut, called Woman Overcoming Recidivism Through Hard work (WORTH) in which the days are packed for the younger women with counseling, classes, and addiction help, giving them a version of parenting they may have lacked. While not enough prisoners have been released from this program to indicate reduced recidivism, prison officials talk about a newfound sense of purpose. Instead of using statistics about arrests or disciplinary infractions as indicators of success, these officials tell stories of individuals gaining

---

7. Chammah, "To Help Young Women."

control of their lives and reconnecting with estranged family members.[8]

Diversity: Being inspired by and borrowing some of the European approaches to prison reform demonstrates the cognitive and cultural diversity in this intervention. Open prisons have been around in Finland, for example since about the 1930s. A few decades ago, Finland had one of the highest rates of imprisonment in Europe. Then, in the 1960s, researchers across the Nordic countries started investigating to what extent punishment really helps reduce crime. The conclusion: it doesn't.[9]

Transparency: The prison system in Kerava, Finland uses open prisons. There aren't any gates, locks, or uniforms. Everyone at the Kerava open prison applied to be there. They earn about eight dollars an hour, have cell phones, do their grocery shopping in town, and get three days of vacation every couple of months. They pay rent to the prison; they can choose to study for a university degree in town instead of working, and they get a subsidy for it; they sometimes take supervised camping and fishing trips.

Integrity: "There is no idea that we are locking people up for the rest of their lives," says Tapio Lappi-Seppälä, head of the Institute of Criminology at the University of Helsinki, "because if that's the case, you really should invest and make sure that there is the possibility of rehabilitation." Inmates

---

8. Ibid.

9. Rae Ellen Bichell, "In Finland's 'Open Prisons," Inmates Have the Keys," PRI, April 15, 2015, *https://www.pri.org/stories/2015-04-15/finlands-open-prisons-inmates-have-keys.*

know it wouldn't be hard to escape. "You can go if you want," Hannu Kallio, a convicted drug smuggler says. "But if you escape, you go back to jail. Better to be here."[10]

---

10. Ibid.

WHAT ABOUT ME? IMAGINE YOUR LIFE BASED ON DIGNITY

Dignity is the source of priceless power—it enables us to develop mutually beneficial connections to others and to create positive change in our relationships.
—*Donna Hicks*

When I was fifteen years old, after graduating from high school in Jamaica, I travelled five thousand miles to the other side of the world to attend a school in Edinburgh, Scotland. It was then a boys' school that allowed around twenty girls in the final two years. Four hundred boys, twenty girls, and I was the only black girl there—one of two black students in the whole school. And the only Jamaican. The first few weeks and months were filled with a deluge of questions from my new Scottish friends, many of which frankly astonished me: "How did you learn to speak English so quickly?" "Are there cars in Jamaica?" Where did you get your clothes?" And my favorite was when they would touch my hair and exclaim, "Beth, your hair defies gravity!" In the midst of all this, as I tried to make sense of my experience there, I found myself grappling with questions of visibility. Do they even see me? See my story? See who I am and all of who I am? How do I even see myself?

Yes, there is important and necessary work in striving to look again at the dignity in others. But what about those same questions of visibility, of looking again, being shifted to ourselves? Have you ever felt invisible? It has been my experience that feeling invisible transcends race, gender, age, ability, ethnicity, status, and education. But we cannot control what others see or how they see. We can control how we see ourselves. And regarding ourselves with dignity is powerful. Often, we are so consumed by our work, and even our friends and families, that we forget to shift the gaze on ourselves, as individuals and human beings. Imagine what it would be like to increase our capacity to genuinely see and embrace our own value and worth—physically, emotionally, intellectually, and spiritually. After all, we all yearn to be seen, to be respected, to be recognized and valued. What if we were to do that for ourselves and not depend on others?

As I have presented DIGNITY to varying communities, inevitably someone will ask at the end, "What about me?" How do I see my own dignity? How can I apply the tenets of DIGNITY to my own life? Creating authentic communities is certainly the focus of DIGNITY, but authentic people make up authentic communities. If we don't bring our best selves to our work and our relationships we're less likely to engage. Less likely to be mobilized and to mobilize others around what matters most. This approach increases our capacities to grow and evolve and become the people we are meant to be. My hope for this book is to increase the capacity for communities to embrace dignity in a new way, and to leverage it in the journey towards authenticity. My hope for this epilogue is to increase our capacity as individuals to embrace our own dignity and, too, strive towards living more authentic lives, where what we dream becomes our lived reality.

So how do we do this? So glad you asked! DIGNITY can also be applied to our lives. As you know by now, the lens is not a linear one and can start at any point. I will model that for you and begin the DIGNITY journey with Yield. Each strategy points to a series of questions and choices. They are opportunities to be reflective about who we are and what we value.

Let's begin.

Yield: What do you see for yourself? What do you envision? What do you want out of this self-dignity? Of this looking inwards? Work-life balance? More joy? More focus? More of an ability to be flexible and open? To build patience? Less anxiety? More faith? To be equipped with new skills? What do you want to be different? And to the stay the same? What do you want your efforts to yield? Identify your desired outcomes for this next season of your life.

Identity: Who am I today? Where have I come from? What is my rhythm? What feels good to me? What are my strengths and my vulnerabilities? Not your weaknesses, but vulnerabilities. These exist at a gut level. The things that make your belly churn and your heart race. These are often the parts of our stories we desperately try to hide. What are my triggers? What are my struggles? What gives me fire? What gives my life purpose? Take the time to do some reflection, recognizing that what gives our lives meaning and direction is influenced by the specific moment in our life journey. You know yourself best. Listen to that inner voice. You know what you value and what feels most like you.

Transparency: Know your story. Tell your story. Our stories make us who we are, and who we will become. There is not only power in giving language to our stories, there is power in owning our stories, and even writing new endings. In DIGNITY, we own all parts of our stories. Even the parts that we deem too terrible, embarrassing, or shameful to speak. What do we do with those parts? We share them. In sharing we can shed light in the darkness and healing , or forgiveness, or friendship or a new way out, a resolution can be revealed. We can build community around our story. Even if that community is you and one other person, or a stranger with a listening ear, or frankly a piece of paper that absorbs the ink of a focused pen controlled by you. According to Brené Brown, shame expert and researcher, shame derives its power from being unspeakable; shame thrives in silence.[1] Shame keeps us from telling our own stories and prevents us from listening to others tell their stories. But the good news is that language and story bring light to shame and destroy it and then we can truly be set free. Healing, forgiveness, true joy, living abundantly, being fully alive begin by telling the untold stories.

Nurture: How can I nurture, feed, and support, my dream? What choices do I need to make in order to get where I want to go? These are conscious choices that may be so much in conflict with how I am living now, and that bring about different outcomes. These choices are not easy. They may feel uncomfortable and foreign, and even may produce some anxiety. These choices may be necessary but know that any anxiety that comes along with these choices should not feel destructive and consuming, but rather interesting and healthy. The purpose of change is not to be destructive. These choices should be life-giving and energizing. Remain curious and open to new ways of being. What choices do I need to make?

Integrity: Am I doing what I say I am doing? How many times do we say we want to do something differently—lose weight, or

---

1. Brené Brown, *Daring Greatly: How the Courage to Be Vulnerable Transforms the Way We Live* (New York: Penguin Random House, 2012), 82.

gain weight, for that matter; be a stronger communicator; learn new skills that will benefit our work—but don't actually take the steps to do what we say we are committed to? Integrity is about holding ourselves accountable to the things we say we value. It's about consistency. Authenticity. Making choices that reflect who you are and the values you uphold. But be kind to yourself. Embrace your contradictions. Because they do exist. Sometimes we will have to choose competing values. There will be loss. Sometimes we have to sacrifice one value to elevate another. And that is okay. Just know why, be aware and embrace these contradictions. Doing so doesn't take away from the progress towards your aspirations and dreams. It actually emboldens and encourages you to keep going and you may even discover new capacities and competencies along the way.

Growth: Undergirding this entire DIGNITY journey is the ability to grow in our capacity to develop new competencies. To behave differently. To acquire new skills. To gain new confidence. To make some mistakes, to take new risks, and to experiment carefully. To be willing to see our failures or missteps as learning opportunities. To be willing to be comfortable being uncomfortable. Growth is also knowing when to pull back because you're entering a danger zone. Growth is feeling incompetent but willing to keep on trying, not seeing the next step but still being willing to put your foot out. Growth is increasing our confidence in our own capacity for change. It is fearing less, trusting and believing more and recalibrating our expectations.

Diversity: We all have dignity, but we are all different. Embrace your unique path. No need for comparisons. Embrace what is yours. There is no prescriptive way to get to the outcomes you see in your mind's eye, there are only descriptive ways and you are at the center. You are in control of creating and imagining and nurturing and growing the parts of you that already reside in you, to make what you want a reality. Also remain open to those around you. Be curious about learning new perspectives and new ways of being. Embrace the differences around you, that's how we learn and how we distinguish what works best for us.

And that is DIGNITY! Don't forget yourself. Look and look again at your own dignity. You matter. Your story matters. "We all have the same dark secrets and the same bright hopes. We come from the same place and are headed in the same direction. Above everything else maybe, we all want to be known by each other and to know each other."[2] More than anything, you are worth it. When you've done all this, know that you will have new eyes. Your own vision will become clearer. Your dignity will shine through in a new way and you will see the dignity in others in a new light. It's not what you look at that matters. It's what you see.

---

2. Frederick Buechner, *Beyond Words: Daily Readings in the ABCs of Faith* (New York: HarperCollins, 2004), 52.